P9-AGH-963

DATE DUE

OUR FOREIGNERS

TEXTBOOK EDITION

∴

THE CHRONICLES
OF AMERICA SERIES
ALLEN JOHNSON
EDITOR

GERHARD R. LOMER
CHARLES W. JEFFERYS
ASSISTANT EDITORS

OUR FOREIGNERS

A CHRONICLE OF
AMERICANS IN THE MAKING
BY SAMUEL P. ORTH

NEW HAVEN: YALE UNIVERSITY PRESS
TORONTO: GLASGOW, BROOK & CO.
LONDON: HUMPHREY MILFORD
OXFORD UNIVERSITY PRESS

Copyright, 1920, by Yale University Press

CONTENTS

OUR FOREIGNERS

∴

CHAPTER I

OPENING THE DOOR

Long before men awoke to the vision of America, the Old World was the scene of many stupendous migrations. One after another, the Goths, the Huns, the Saracens, the Turks, and the Tatars, by the sheer tidal force of their numbers threatened to engulf the ancient and medieval civilization of Europe. But neither in the motives prompting them nor in the effect they produced, nor yet in the magnitude of their numbers, will such migrations bear comparison with the great exodus of European peoples which in the course of three centuries has made the United States of America. That movement of races — first across the sea and then across the land to yet another sea, which set in with the English occupation of Virginia in 1607 and which

has continued from that day to this an almost cease-
less stream of millions of human beings seeking in
the New World what was denied them in the Old —
has no parallel in history.

It was not until the seventeenth century that the
door of the wilderness of North America was opened
by Englishmen; but, if we are interested in the circumstances and ideas which turned Englishmen
thither, we must look back into the wonderful sixteenth century — and even into the fifteenth, for
it was only five or six years after the great Chris-
topher's discovery, that the Cabots, John and Se-
bastian, raised the Cross of St. George on the North
American coast.   Two generations later, when the
New World was pouring its treasure into the lap of
Spain and when all England was pulsating with
the new and noble life of the Elizabethan Age, the
sea captains of the Great Queen challenged the
Spanish monarch, defeated his Great Armada, and
unfurled the English flag, symbol of a changing era,
in every sea.

The political and economic thought of the sixteenth century was conducive to imperial expansion.   The feudal fragments of kingdoms were being fused into a true nationalism.   It was the day
of the mercantilists, when gold and silver were

given a grotesquely exaggerated place in the national economy and self-sufficiency was deemed to be the goal of every great nation. Freed from the restraint of rivals, the nation sought to produce its own raw material, control its own trade, and carry its own goods in its own ships to its own markets. This economic doctrine appealed with peculiar force to the people of England. England was very far from being self-sustaining. She was obliged to import salt, sugar, dried fruits, wines, silks, cotton, potash, naval stores, and many other necessary commodities. Even of the fish which formed a staple food on the English workman's table, two-thirds of the supply was purchased from the Dutch. Moreover, wherever English traders sought to take the products of English industry, mostly woolen goods, they were met by handicaps — tariffs, Sound dues, monopolies, exclusions, retaliations, and even persecutions.

So England was eager to expand under her own flag. With the fresh courage and buoyancy of youth she fitted out ships and sent forth expeditions. And while she shared with the rest of the Europeans the vision of India and the Orient, her "gentlemen adventurers" were not long in seeing the possibilities that lay concealed beyond the inviting harbors, the navigable rivers, and the forest-covered valleys of North America. With a willing heart they believed their quaint chronicler, Richard Hakluyt, when he declared that America could bring "*as great a profit to the Realme of England as the Indes to the King of Spain*," that "*golde, silver, copper, leade and perales in aboundaunce*" had been found there: also "*precious stones, as turquoises and emauraldes; spices and drugges; silke worms fairer than ours in Europe; white and red cotton; infinite multitude of all kind of fowles; excellent vines in many places for wines; the soyle apte to beare olyves for oyle; all kinds of fruites; all kindes of odoriferous trees and date trees, cypresses, and cedars; and in New-foundelande aboundaunce of pines and firr trees to make mastes and deale boards, pitch, tar, rosen; hempe for cables and cordage; and upp within the Graunde Baye excedinge quantitie of all kinde of precious furres.*" Such a catalogue of resources led him to conclude that "*all the commodities of our olde decayed and daungerous trades in all Europe, Africa and Asia haunted by us, may in short space and for little or nothinge, in a manner be had in that part of America which lieth between 30 and 60 degrees of northerly latitude.*"

Even after repeated expeditions had discounted

the exuberant optimism of this description, the Englishmen's faith did not wane. While for many years there lurked in the mind of the Londoner, the hope that some of the products of the Levant might be raised in the fertile valleys of Virginia, the practical English temperament none the less began promptly to appease itself with the products of the vast forests, the masts, the tar and pitch, the furs; with the fish from the coast waters, the abundant cod, herring, and mackerel; nor was it many years before tobacco, indigo, sugar, cotton, maize, and other commodities brought to the merchants of England a great American commerce.

The first attempts to found colonies in the country by Sir Humphrey Gilbert and Sir Walter Raleigh were pitiable failures. But the settlement on the James in 1607 marked the beginning of a nation. What sort of nation? What race of people? Sir Walter Raleigh, with true English tenacity, had said after learning of the collapse of his own colony, "I shall yet live to see it an English nation." The new nation certainly was English in its foundation, whatever may be said of its superstructure. Virginia, New England, Maryland, the Carolinas, New Jersey, Pennsylvania, and Georgia were begun by Englishmen; and New England, Virginia, and Maryland remained almost entirely English throughout the seventeenth century and well into the eighteenth. These colonies reproduced, in so far as their strange and wild surroundings permitted, the towns, the estates, and the homes of Englishmen of that day. They were organized and governed by Englishmen under English customs and laws; and the Englishman's constitutional liberties were their boast until the colonists wrote these rights and privileges into a constitution of their own. "Foreigners" began early to straggle into the colonies. But not until the eighteenth century was well under way did they come in appreciable numbers, and even then the great bulk of these non-English newcomers were from the British Isles — of Welsh, Scotch, Irish, and Scotch-Irish extraction.

These colonies took root at a time when profound social and religious changes were occurring in England. Churchmen and dissenters were at war with each other; autocracy was struggling to survive the representative system; and agrarianism was contending with a newly created capitalism for economic supremacy. The old order was changing. In vain were attempts made to stay progress by labor laws and poor laws and corn laws. The laws rather served to fill the highways with vagrants, vagabonds, mendicants, beggars, and worse. There was a general belief that the country was over-populated. For the restive, the discontented, the ambitious, as well as for the undesirable surplus, the new colonies across the Atlantic provided a welcome outlet.

To the southern plantations were lured those to whom land-owning offered not only a means of livelihood but social distinction. As word was brought back of the prosperity of the great estates and of the limitless areas awaiting cultivation, it tempted in substantial numbers those who were dissatisfied with their lot: the yeoman who saw no escape from the limitations of his class, either for himself or for his children; the younger son who disdained trade but was too poor to keep up family pretensions; professional men, lawyers, and doctors, even clergymen, who were ambitious to become landed gentlemen; all these felt the irresistible call of the New World.

The northern colonies were, on the other hand, settled by townfolk, by that sturdy middle class which had wedged its way socially between the aristocracy and the peasantry, which asserted itself politically in the Cromwellian Commonwealth and later became the industrial master of trade and manufacture. These hard-headed dissenters founded New England. They built towns and almost immediately developed a profitable trade and manufacture. With a goodly sprinkling of university men among them, they soon had a college of their own. Indeed, Harvard graduated its first class as early as 1642.

Supplementing these pioneers, came mechanics and artisans eager to better their condition. Of the serving class, only a few came willingly. These were the "free-willers" or "redemptioners," who sold their services usually for a term of five years to pay for their passage money. But the great mass of unskilled labor necessary to clear the forests and do the other hard work so plentiful in a pioneer land came to America under duress. Kidnaping or "spiriting" achieved the perfection of a fine art under the second Charles. Boys and girls of the poorer classes, those wretched waifs who thronged the streets of London and other towns, were hustled on board ships and virtually sold into slavery for a term of years. It is said that in 1670 alone ten thousand persons were thus kidnaped; and one kidnaper testified in 1671 that he had sent five hundred persons a year to the colonies for twelve years and another that he had sent 840 in one year.

Transportation of the idle poor was another common source for providing servants. In 1663 an act was passed by Parliament empowering Justices of the Peace to send rogues, vagrants, and "sturdy beggars" to the colonies. These men belonged to the class of the unfortunate rather than the vicious and were the product of a passing state of society, though criminals also were deported. Virginia and other colonies vigorously protested against this practice, but their protests were ignored by the Crown. When, however, it is recalled that in those years the list of capital offenses was appalling in length, that the larceny of a few shillings was punishable by death, that many of the victims were deported because of religious differences and political offenses, then the stigma of crime is erased. And one does not wonder that some of these transported persons rose to places of distinction and honor in the colonies and that many of them became respected citizens. Maryland, indeed, recruited her schoolmasters from among their ranks.

Indentured service was an institution of that time, as was slavery. The lot of the indentured servant was not ordinarily a hard one. Here and there masters were cruel and inhuman. But in a new country where hands were so few and work so abundant, it was wisdom to be tolerant and humane. Servants who had worked out their time usually became tenants or freeholders, often moving to other colonies and later to the interior beyond the "fall line," where they became pioneers in their turn.

The most important and influential influx of non-English stock into the colonies was the copious stream of Scotch-Irish. Frontier life was not a new experience to these hardy and remarkable people. Ulster, when they migrated thither from Scotland in the early part of the seventeenth century, was a wild moorland, and the Irish were more than unfriendly neighbors. Yet these transplanted Scotch changed the fens and mires into fields and gardens; in three generations they had built flourishing towns and were doing a thriving manufacture in linens and woolens. Then England, in her mercantilist blindness, began to pass legislation that aimed to cut off these fabrics from English competition. Soon thousands of Ulster artisans were out of work. Nor was their religion immune from English attack, for these Ulstermen were Presbyterians. These civil, religious, and economic persecutions thereupon drove to America an ethnic strain that has had an influence upon the character of the nation far out of proportion to its relative numbers. In the long list of leaders in American politics and enterprise and in every branch of learning, Scotch-Irish names are common.

There had been some trade between Ulster and the colonies, and a few Ulstermen had settled on the eastern shore of Maryland and in Virginia before the close of the seventeenth century. Between 1714 and 1720, fifty-four ships arrived in Boston with immigrants from Ireland. They were carefully scrutinized by the Puritan exclusionists. Cotton Mather wrote in his diary on August 7, 1718: "But what shall be done for the great number of people that are transporting themselves thither from ye North of Ireland?" And John Winthrop, speaking of twenty ministers and their congregations that were expected the same year, said, "I wish their coming so over do not prove fatall in the End." They were not welcome, and had, evidently, no intention of burdening the towns. Most of them promptly moved on beyond the New England settlements.

The great mass of Scotch-Irish, however, came to Pennsylvania, and in such large numbers that James Logan, the Secretary of the Province, wrote to the Proprietors in 1729: "It looks as if Ireland is to send all its inhabitants hither, for last week not less than six ships arrived, and every day two or three arrive also."[1] These colonists did not remain in the towns but, true to their traditions, pushed on to the frontier. They found their way over the mountain trails into the western part of the colony; they pushed southward along the fertile plateaus that terrace the Blue Ridge Mountains and offer a natural highway to the South; into Virginia, where they possessed themselves of the beautiful Shenandoah Valley; into Maryland and the Carolinas; until the whole western frontier, from Georgia to New York and from Massachusetts to Maine, was the skirmish line of the Scotch-Irish taking possession of the wilderness.

The rebellions of the Pretenders in Scotland in 1715 and 1745 and the subsequent break-up of the clan system produced a considerable migration to the colonies from both the Highlands and the Lowlands. These new colonists settled largely in the Carolinas and in Maryland. The political

---

[1] In 1773 and 1774 over thirty thousand came. In the latter year Benjamin Franklin estimated the population of Pennsylvania at 350,000, of which number one-third was thought to be Scotch-Irish. John Fiske states that half a million, all told, arrived in the colonies before 1776, "making not less than one-sixth part of our population at the time of the Revolution."

prisoners, of whom there were many in consequence of the rebellions, were sold into service, usually for a term of fourteen years.   In Pennsylvania the Welsh founded a number of settlements in the neighborhood of Philadelphia.   There were Irish servants in all the colonies and in Maryland many Irish Catholics joined their fellow Catholics from England.

In 1683 a group of religious refugees from the Rhineland founded Germantown, near Philadelphia.   Soon other German communities were started in the neighboring counties.   Chief among these German sectarians were the Mennonites, frequently called the German Quakers, so nearly did their religious peculiarities match those of the followers of Penn; the Dunkers, a Baptist sect, who seem to have come from Germany boot and baggage, leaving not one of their number behind; and the Moravians, whose missionary zeal and gentle demeanor have made them beloved in many lands. The peculiar religious devotions of the sectarians still left them time to cultivate their inclination for literature and music.   There were a few distinguished scholars among them and some of the finest examples of early American books bear the imprint of their presses.

This modest beginning of the German invasion was soon followed by more imposing additions. The repeated strategic devastations of the Rhenish Palatinate during the French and Spanish wars reduced the peasantry to beggary, and the medieval social stratification of Germany reduced them to virtual serfdom, from which America offered emancipation. Queen Anne invited the harassed peasants of this region to come to England, whence they could be transferred to America. Over thirty thousand took advantage of the opportunity in the years 1708 and 1709.[1] Some of them found occupation in England and others in Ireland, but the majority migrated, some to New York, where they settled in the Mohawk Valley, others to the Carolinas, but far more to Pennsylvania, where, with an instinct born of generations of contact with the soil, they sought out the most promising areas in the limestone valleys of the eastern part of that colony, cleared the land, built their solid homes and ample barns, and clung to their language, customs, and religion so tenaciously that to this day their descendants are called "Pennsylvania Dutch."

After 1717 multitudes of German peasants were

[1] John Fiske: *The Dutch and Quaker Colonies in America*, vol. II, p. 351.

lured to America by unscrupulous agents called "new-landers" or "soul-stealers," who, for a commission paid by the shipmaster, lured the peasant to sell his belongings, scrape together or borrow what he could, and migrate. The agents and captains then saw to it that few arrived in Philadelphia out of debt. As a result the immigrants were sold to "soul-drivers," who took them to the interior and indentured them to farmers, usually of their own race. These redemptioners, as they were called, served from three to five years and generally received fifty acres of land at the expiration of their service.

On the revocation of the Edict of Nantes by Louis XIV in 1685 French Protestants fled in vast numbers to England and to Holland. Thence many of them found their way to America, but very few came hither directly from France. South Carolina, Virginia, New York, Rhode Island, and Massachusetts were favored by those noble refugees, who included in their numbers not only skilled artisans and successful merchants but distinguished scholars and professional men in whose veins flowed some of the best blood of France. They readily identified themselves with the industries and aspirations of the colonies and at once became leaders in the professional and business life in their communities. In Boston, in Charleston, in New York, and in other commercial centers, the names of streets, squares, and public buildings attest their prominence in trade and politics. Few names are more illustrious than those of Paul Revere, Peter Faneuil, and James Bowdoin of Massachusetts; John Jay, Nicholas Bayard, Stephen DeLancey of New York; Elias Boudinot of New Jersey; Henry Laurens and Francis Marion of South Carolina. Like the Scotch-Irish, these French Protestants and their descendants have distinguished themselves for their capacity for leadership.

The Jews came early to New York, and as far back as 1691 they had a synagogue in Manhattan. The civil disabilities then so common in Europe were not enforced against them in America, except that they could not vote for members of the legislature. As that body itself declared in 1737, the Jews did not possess the parliamentary franchise in England, and no special act had endowed them with this right in the colonies. The earliest representatives of this race in America came to New Amsterdam with the Dutch and were nearly all Spanish and Portuguese Jews, who had found refuge in Holland after their wholesale expulsion from the Iberian peninsula in 1492. Rhode Island, too, and Pennsylvania had a substantial Jewish population. The Jews settled characteristically in the towns and soon became a factor in commercial enterprise. It is to be noted that they contributed liberally to the patriot cause in the Revolution.

While the ships bearing these many different stocks were sailing westward, England did not gain possession of the whole Atlantic seaboard without contest. The Dutch came to Manhattan in 1623 and for fifty years held sway over the imperial valley of the Hudson. It was a brief interval, as history goes, but it was long enough to stamp upon the town of Manhattan the cosmopolitan character it has ever since maintained. Into its liberal and congenial atmosphere were drawn Jews, Moravians, and Anabaptists; Scotch Presbyterians and English Nonconformists; Waldenses from Piedmont and Huguenots from France. The same spirit that made Holland the lenient host to political and religious refugees from every land in that restive age characterized her colony and laid the foundations of the great city of today. England had to wrest from the Dutch their ascendancy in New Netherland, where they split in twain the great English colonies of New England and of the South and controlled the magnificent harbor at the mouth of the Hudson, which has since become the water gate of the nation.

While the English were thus engaged in establishing themselves on the coast, the French girt them in by a strategic circle of forts and trading posts reaching from Acadia, up the St. Lawrence, around the Great Lakes, and down the valley of the Mississippi, with outposts on the Ohio and other important confluents. When, after the final struggle between France and Britain for world empire, France retired from the North American continent, she left to England all her possessions east of the Mississippi, with the exception of a few insignificant islands in the Gulf of St. Lawrence and the West Indies; and to Spain she ceded New Orleans and her vast claims beyond the great river.

Thus from the first, the lure of the New World beckoned to many races, and to every condition of men. By the time that England's dominion spread over half the northern continent, her colonies were no longer merely English. They were the most cosmopolitan areas in the world. A few European cities had at times been cities of refuge, but New York and Philadelphia were more than mere temporary shelters to every creed. Nowhere else could so many tongues be heard as in a stroll down Broadway to the Battery. No European commonwealths embraced in their citizenry one-half the ethnic diversity of the Carolinas or of Pennsylvania. And within the wide range of his American domains, the English King could point to one spot or another and say: "Here the Spaniards have built a chaste and beautiful mission; here the French have founded a noble city; here my stubborn Roundheads have planted a whole nest of commonwealths; here my Dutch neighbors thought they stole a march on me, but I forestalled them; this valley is filled with Germans, and that plateau is covered with Scotch-Irish, while the Swedes have taken possession of all this region." And with a proud gesture he could add, "But everywhere they read their laws in the King's English and acknowledge my sovereignty."

Against the shifting background of history these many races of diverse origin played their individual parts, each contributing its essential characteristics to the growing complex of a new order of society in America. So on this stage, broad as the western world, we see these men of different strains subduing a wilderness and welding its diverse parts into a great nation, stretching out the

eager hand of exploration for yet more land, bringing with arduous toil the ample gifts of sea and forest to the townsfolk, hewing out homesteads in the
savage wilderness, laboring faithfully at forge and
shipyard and loom, bartering in the market place,
putting the fear of God into their children and the
fear of their own strong right arm into him whosoever sought to oppress them, be he Red Man with
his tomahawk or English King with his Stamp Act.

CHAPTER II

IN the history of a word we may frequently find a fragment, sometimes a large section, of universal history. This is exemplified in the term American, a name which, in the phrase of George Washington, "must always exalt the pride of patriotism" and which today is proudly borne by a hundred million people. There is no obscurity about the origin of the name America. It was suggested for the New World in 1507 by Martin Waldseemüller, a German geographer at the French college of Saint-Dié. In that year this savant printed a tract, with a map of the world or *mappemonde*, recognizing the dubious claims of discovery set up by Amerigo Vespucci and naming the new continent after him. At first applied only to South America, the name was afterwards extended to mean the northern continent as well; and in time the whole New World, from the Frozen Ocean to the Land of Fire, came to be called America.

Inevitably the people who achieved a preponderating influence in the new continent came to be called Americans. Today the name American everywhere signifies belonging to the United States, and a citizen of that country is called an American. This unquestionably is geographically anomalous, for the neighbors of the United States, both north and south, may claim an equal share in the term. Ethnically, the only real Americans are the Indian descendants of the aboriginal races. But it is futile to combat universal usage: the World War has clinched the name upon the inhabitants of the United States. The American army, the American navy, American physicians and nurses, American food and clothing — these are phrases with a definite geographical and ethnic meaning which neither academic ingenuity nor race rivalry can erase from the memory of mankind.

This chapter, however, is to discuss the American stock, and it is necessary to look farther back than mere citizenship; for there are millions of American citizens of foreign birth or parentage who, though they are Americans, are clearly not of any American stock.

At the time of the Revolution there was a definite American population, knit together by over two centuries of toil in the hard school of frontier life, inspired by common political purposes, speaking one language, worshiping one God in divers manners, acknowledging one sovereignty, and complying with the mandates of one common law. Through their common experience in subduing the wilderness and in wresting their independence from an obstinate and stupid monarch, the English colonies became a nation. Though they did not fulfill Raleigh's hope and become an English nation, they were much more English than non-English, and these Revolutionary Americans may be called today, without abuse of the term, the original American stock. Though they were a blend of various races, a cosmopolitan admixture of ethnic strains, they were not more varied than the original admixture of blood now called English.

We may, then, properly begin our survey of the racial elements in the United States by a brief scrutiny of this American stock, the parent stem of the American people, the great trunk, whose roots have penetrated deep into the human experience of the past and whose branches have pushed upward and outward until they spread over a whole continent.

The first census of the United States was taken in 1790. More than a hundred years later, in 1909, the Census Bureau published *A Century of Population Growth* in which an attempt was made to ascertain the nationality of those who comprised the population at the taking of the first census. In that census no questions of nativity were asked. This omission is in itself significant of the homogeneity of the population at that time. The only available data, therefore, upon which such a calculation could be made were the surnames of the heads of families preserved in the schedules. A careful analysis of the list disclosed a surprisingly large number of names ostensibly English or British. Fashions in names have changed since then, and many that were so curious, simple, or fantastically compounded as to be later deemed undignified have undergone change or disappeared.[1]

---

[1] Among the names which have quite vanished were those pertaining to household matters, such as Hash, Butter, Waffle, Booze, Frill, Shirt, Lace; or describing human characteristics, as Booby, Dunce, Sallow, Daft, Lazy, Measley, Rude; or parts of the body and its ailments, as Hips, Bones, Chin, Glands, Gout, Corns, Physic; or representing property, as Shingle, Gutters, Pump, Milkhouse, Desk, Mug, Auction, Hose, Tallow. Nature also was drawn upon for a large number of names. The colors Black, Brown, and Gray survive, but Lavender, Tan, and Scarlet have gone out of vogue. Bogs, Hazelgrove, Woodyfield, Oysterbanks, Chestnut, Pinks, Ragbush, Winterberry, Peach, Walnut, Freeze,

Upon this basis the nationality of the white population was distributed among the States in accordance with Table A printed on pages 26–27. Three of the original States are not represented in this table: New Jersey, Delaware, and Georgia. The schedules of the First Census for those States were not preserved. The two new States of Kentucky and Tennessee are also missing from the list. Estimates, however, have been made for these missing States.

For Delaware, the schedules of the Second Census, 1800, survived. As there was little growth and very little change in the composition of the population during this decade, the Census Bureau used the later figures as a basis for calculating the population in 1790. Of three of the missing Southern States the report says: "The composition of the white population of Georgia, Kentucky, and of the district subsequently erected into the State of Tennessee is also unknown; but in view of the fact that Georgia was a distinctly English colony, and that Tennessee and Kentucky were settled largely

---

Coldair, Bear, Tails, Chick, Bantam, Stork, Worm, Snake, and Maggot indicate the simple origin of many names. There were many strange combinations of Christian names and surnames: Peter Wentup, Christy Forgot, Unity Bachelor, Booze Still, Cutlip Hoof, and Wanton Bump left little to the imagination.

TABLE A[1]

Distribution of the white population, 1790, in each state, according to nationality as indicated by names of heads of families

Note: The first column under each State gives the number of persons; the second, the percentage. The asterisk indicates less than one-tenth of one per cent.

NATIONALITY	MAINE		NEW HAMPSHIRE		VERMONT		MASSACHUSETTS	
All Nationalities	96,107	100.0	141,112	100.0	85,072	100.0	373,187	100.0
English	89,515	93.1	132,726	94.1	81,149	95.4	354,528	95.0
Scotch	4,154	4.3	6,648	4.7	2,562	3.0	13,435	3.6
Irish	1,334	1.4	1,346	1.0	597	0.7	3,732	1.0
Dutch	279	0.3	153	0.1	428	0.5	373	0.1
French	115	0.1	142	0.1	153	0.2	746	0.2
German	436	0.5			35	*	75	*
Hebrew	44	*					67	*
All others	230	0.2	97	0.1	148	0.2	231	*

[1] These tables and those on the pages immediately following are taken from *A Century of Population Growth*, issued by the United States Census Bureau in 1908.

NATIONALITY	RHODE ISLAND		CONNECTICUT		NEW YORK		PENNSYLVANIA	
All Nationalities	64,670	100.0	232,236	100.0	314,366	100.0	423,373	100.0
English	62,079	96.0	223,437	96.2	245,901	78.2	249,656	59.0
Scotch	1,976	3.1	6,425	2.8	10,034	3.2	49,567	11.7
Irish	459	0.7	1,589	0.7	2,525	0.8	8,614	2.0
Dutch	19	*	258	0.1	50,600	16.1	2,623	0.6
French	88	0.1	512	0.2	2,424	0.8	2,341	0.6
German	33	0.1	4	*	1,103	0.4	110,357	26.1
Hebrew	9	*	5	*	385	0.1	21	*
All others	7	*	6	*	1,394	0.4	194	*

NATIONALITY	MARYLAND		VIRGINIA		NORTH CAROLINA		SOUTH CAROLINA	
All Nationalities	208,649	100.0	442,117	100.0	289,181	100.0	140,178	100.0
English	175,265	84.0	375,799	85.0	240,309	83.1	115,480	82.4
Scotch	13,562	6.5	31,391	7.1	32,388	11.2	16,447	11.7
Irish	5,008	2.4	8,842	2.0	6,651	2.3	3,576	2.6
Dutch	209	0.1	884	0.2	578	0.2	219	0.2
French	1,460	0.7	2,653	0.6	868	0.3	1,882	1.3
German	12,310	5.9	21,664	4.9	8,097	2.8	2,343	1.7
Hebrew	626	0.3			1	*	85	*
All others	209	0.1	884	0.2	289	0.1	146	0.1

TABLE B

COMPUTED DISTRIBUTION OF WHITE POPULATION, 1790, ACCORDING
TO NATIONALITY, IN EACH STATE FOR WHICH SCHEDULES
ARE MISSING

NATIONALITY	NEW JERSEY		DELAWARE		GEORGIA	
All Nationalities	169,954	100.0	46,310	100.0	52,886	100.0
English	98,620	58.0	39,966	86.3	43,948	83.1
Scotch	13,156	7.7	3,473	7.5	5,923	11.2
Irish	12,099	7.1	1,806	3.9	1,216	2.3
Dutch	21,581	12.7	463	1.0	106	0.2
French	3,565	2.1	232	0.5	159	0.3
German	15,678	9.2	185	0.4	1,481	2.8
All others*	5,255	3.1	185	0.4	53	0.1

NATIONALITY	KENTUCKY		TENNESSEE	
All Nationalities	61,133	100.0	31,913	100.0
English	50,802	83.1	26,519	83.1
Scotch	6,847	11.2	3,574	11.2
Irish	1,406	2.3	734	2.3
Dutch	122	0.2	64	0.2
French	183	0.3	96	0.3
German	1,712	2.8	894	2.8
All others*	61	0.1	32	0.1

* Including Hebrews.

from Virginia and North Carolina, the application
of the North Carolina proportions to the white
population of these three results in what is doubtless an approximation of the actual distribution."

New Jersey presented a more complex problem. Here were Welsh and Swedes, Finns and Danes, as well as French, Dutch, Scotch, Irish, and English. A careful analysis was made of lists of freeholders, and other available sources, in the various counties. The results of these computations in the States from which nc schedules of the First Census survive are given in Table B printed on page 28.

The calculations for the entire country in 1790, based upon the census schedules of the States from which reports are still available and upon estimates for the others are summed up in the following manner:

Number and per cent distribution of the white population, 1790:

Nationality	Number	Per Cent
All Nationalities	3,172,444	100.0
English	2,605,699	82.1
Scotch	221,562	7.0
Irish	61,534	1.9
Dutch	78,959	2.5
French	17,619	0.6
German	176,407	5.6
All others	10,664	0.3

To this method of estimating nationality, it will at once be objected that undue prominence is given to the derivation of the surname, an objection fully understood by those who made the estimate and one which deprives their conclusions of strict scientific verity. In a new country, where the population is in a constant flux and where members of a community composed of one race easily migrate to another part of the country and fall in with people of another race, it is very easy to modify the name to suit new circumstances. We know, for instance, that Isaac Isaacks of Pennsylvania was not a Jew, that the Van Buskirks of New Jersey were German, not Dutch, that D'Aubigné was early shortened into Dabny and Aulnay into Olney. So also many a Brown had been Braun, and several Blacks had once been only Schwartz. Even the universal Smith had absorbed more than one original Schmidt. These rather exceptional cases, however, probably do not vitiate the general conclusion here made as to the British and non-British element in the population of America, for the Dutch, the German, the French, and the Swedish cognomens are characteristically different from the British. But the differentiation between Irish, Welsh, Scotch, Scotch-Irish, and English names is infinitely more difficult. The Scotch-Irish particularly have challenged the conclusions reached by the Census Bureau. They claim a much larger proportion of the original bulk of our population than the seven per cent included under the heading Scotch. Henry Jones Ford considers the conclusions as far as they pertain to the Scotch-Irish as "fallacious and untrustworthy." "Many Ulster names," he says,[1] "are also common English names. . . . Names classed as Scotch or Irish were probably mostly those of Scotch-Irish families. . . . The probability is that the English proportion should be much smaller and that the Scotch-Irish, who are not included in the Census Bureau's classification, should be much larger than the combined proportions allotted to the Scotch and the Irish."

Whatever may be the actual proportions of these British elements, as revealed by a study of the patronymics of the population at the time of American independence, the fact that the ethnic stock was overwhelmingly British stands out most prominently. We shall never know the exact ratios between the Scotch and the English, the Welsh and the Irish blended in this hardy, self-assertive, and fecund strain. But we do know that the language, the political institutions, and the common law as practiced and established in London had a

[1] *The Scotch-Irish in America*, pp. 219-20.

predominating influence on the destinies of the United States. While the colonists drifted far from the religious establishments of the mother country and found her commercial policies unendurable and her political hauteur galling, they nevertheless retained those legal and institutional forms which remain the foundation of Anglo-Saxon life.

For nearly half a century the American stock remained almost entirely free from foreign admixture. It is estimated that between 1790 and 1820 only 250,000 immigrants came to America, and of these the great majority came after the War of 1812. The white population of the United States in 1820 was 7,862,166. Ten years later it had risen to 10,537,378. This astounding increase was almost wholly due to the fecundity of the native stock. The equitable balance between the sexes, the ease of acquiring a home, the vigorous pioneer environment, and the informal frontier social conditions all encouraged large families. Early marriages were encouraged. Bachelors and unmarried women were rare. Girls were matrons at twenty-five and grandmothers at forty. Three generations frequently dwelt in one homestead. Families of five persons were the rule; families of eight or ten were common, while families of fourteen or fifteen did not elicit surprise. It was the father's ambition to leave a farm to every son and, if the neighborhood was too densely settled easily to permit this, there was the West — always the West.

This was a race of nation builders. No sooner had he made the Declaration of Independence a reality than the eager pathfinder turned his face towards the setting sun and, prompted by the instincts of conquest, he plunged into the wilderness. Within a few years western New York and Pennsylvania were settled; Kentucky achieved statehood in 1792 and Tennessee four years later, soon to be followed by Mississippi in 1817 and Alabama in 1819. The great Northwest Territory yielded Ohio in 1802, Indiana in 1816, Illinois in 1818, and Michigan in 1837. Beyond the Mississippi the empire of Louisiana doubled the original area of the Republic; Louisiana came into statehood in 1812 and Missouri in 1821. Texas, Oregon, and the fruits of the Mexican War extended its confines to the Western Sea. Incredibly swift as was this march of the Stars, the American pioneer was always in advance.

The pathfinders were virtually all of American stock. The States admitted to the Union prior to 1840 were not only founded by them; they were almost wholly settled by them. When the influx of foreigners began in the thirties, they found all the trails already blazed, the trading posts established, and the first terrors of the wilderness dispelled. They found territories already metamorphosed into States, counties organized, cities established. Schools, churches, and colleges preceded the immigrants who were settlers and not strictly pioneers. The entire territory ceded by the Treaty of 1783 was appropriated in large measure by the American before the advent of the European immigrant.

Washington, with a ring of pride, said in 1796 that the native population of America was "filling the western part of the State of New York and the country on the Ohio with their own surplusage." And James Madison in 1821 wrote that New England, "which has sent out such a continued swarm to other parts of the Union for a number of years, has continued at the same time, as the census shows, to increase in population although it is well known that it has received but comparatively few emigrants from any quarter." Beyond the Mississippi, Louisiana, with its creole population, was feeling the effect of American migration.

A strange restlessness, of the race rather than of the individual, possessed the American frontiersman. He moved from one locality to another, but always westward, like some new migratory species that had willingly discarded the instinct for returning. He never took the back trail. A traveler, writing in 1791 from the Ohio Valley, rather superficially observed that "the Americans are lazy and bored, often moving from place to place for the sake of change; in the thirty years that the [western] Pennsylvania neighborhood has been settled, it has changed owners two or three times. The sight of money will tempt any American to sell and off he goes to a new country." Foreign observers of that time constantly allude to this universal and inexplicable restiveness. It was obviously not laziness, for pioneering was a man's task; nor boredom, for the frontier was lonely and neighbors were far apart. It was an ever-present dissatisfaction that drove this perpetual conqueror onward — a mysterious impulse, the urge of vague and unfulfilled desires. He went forward with a conquering ambition in his heart; he believed he was the forerunner of a great National Destiny. Crude rhymes of the day voice this feeling:

So shall the nation's pioneer go joyful on his way,
To wed Penobscot water to San Francisco Bay.
The mighty West shall bless the East, and sea
    shall answer sea,

And mountain unto mountain call, praise God,
   for we are free!

Again a popular chorus of the pathfinder rang:

> Then o'er the hills in legions, boys;
>   Fair freedom's star
> Points to the sunset regions, boys,
>   Ha, Ha, Ha-ha!

Many a New Englander cleared a farm in western New York, Ohio, or Indiana, before settling finally in Wisconsin, Iowa, or Minnesota, whence he sent his sons on to Dakota, Montana, Oregon, and California. From Tennessee and Kentucky large numbers moved into southern Ohio, Indiana, Illinois, and across the river into Missouri, Arkansas, Louisiana, and Texas. Abraham Lincoln's father was one of these pioneers and tried his luck in various localities in Kentucky, Indiana, and Illinois.

Nor had the movement ceased after a century of continental exploitation. Hamlin Garland in his notable autobiography, *A Son of the Middle Border*, brings down to our own day the evidence of this native American restiveness. His parents came of New England extraction, but settled in Wisconsin. His father, after his return from the Civil War, moved to Iowa, where he was scarcely ensconced before an opportunity came to sell his place. The family then pushed out farther upon the Iowa prairie, where they "broke" a farm from the primeval turf. Again, in his ripe age, the father found the urge revive and under this impulse he moved again, this time to Dakota, where he remained long enough to transform a section of prairie into wheat land before he took the final stage of his western journeyings to southern California. Here he was surrounded by neighbors whose migration had been not unlike his own, and to the same sunny region another relative found his way "by way of a long trail through Iowa, Dakota, Montana, Oregon, and North California."

When the last frontier had vanished, it was seen that men of this American stock had penetrated into every valley, traversed every plain, and explored every mountain pass from Atlantic to Pacific. They organized every territory and prepared each for statehood. It was the enterprise of these sons and grandsons and great-grandsons of the Revolutionary Americans, obeying the restless impulse of a pioneer race, who spread a network of settlements and outposts over the entire land and prepared it for the immigrant invasion from Europe. Owing to this influx of foreigners, the American stock has become mingled with other strains, especially those from Great Britain.

The Census Bureau estimated that in 1900 there were living in the United States approximately thirty-five million white people who were descended from persons enumerated in 1790. If these thirty-five million were distributed by nationality according to the proportions estimated for 1790, the result would appear as follows:

English	28,735,000
Scotch	2,450,000
Irish	665,000
Dutch	875,000
French	210,000
German	1,960,000
All others	105,000

In 1900 there were also thirty-two million descendants of white persons who had come to the United States after the First Census, yet of these over twenty million were either foreign born or the children of persons born abroad. If this ratio of increase remained the same, the American stock would apparently maintain its own, even in the midst of twentieth century immigration. But the birth rate of the foreign stock, especially among the recent comers, is much higher than of the native American stock. Conditions have so changed that, according to the Census, the American people "have concluded that they are only about one-half as well able to rear children — at any rate, without personal sacrifice — under the conditions prevailing in 1900 as their predecessors proved themselves to be under the conditions which prevailed in 1790."

The difficulty of ascertaining ethnic influences increases immeasurably when we pass from the physical to the mental realm. There are subtle interplays of delicate forces and reactions from environment which no one can measure. Leadership nevertheless is the gift of but few races; and in the United States eminence in business, in statecraft, in letters and learning can with singular directness be traced in a preponderating proportion to this American stock.

In 1891 Henry Cabot Lodge published an essay on *The Distribution of Ability in the United States*,[1] based upon the 15,514 names in Appleton's *Cyclopædia of American Biography* (1887). He "treated as immigrants all persons who came to the United States after the adoption of the Constitution," and on this division he found 14,243 "Americans"

---

[1] See *The Century Magazine*, September, 1891, and Lodge's *Historical and Political Essays*, 1892.

and 1271 "immigrants," distributed racially as
follows:

AMERICANS		IMMIGRANTS	
English	10,376	English	345
Scotch-Irish	1439	German	245
German	659	Irish	200
Huguenot	589	Scotch	151
Scotch	436	Scotch-Irish	88
Dutch	336	French	68
Welsh	159	Canadian and	
Irish	109	British Colonial	60
French	85	Scandinavian	18
Scandinavian	31	Welsh	16
Spanish	7	Belgian	15
Italian	7	Swiss	15
Swiss	5	Dutch	14
Greek	3	Polish	13
Russian	1	Hungarian	11
Polish	1	Italian	10
		Greek	3
		Russian	2
		Spanish	1
		Portuguese	1

Of the total number of individuals selected, a
large number were chosen by the editors as being of
enough importance to entitle them to a small portrait in the text, and fifty-eight persons who had
achieved some unusual distinction were accorded

a full-page portrait. These, however, represented achievement rather than ability, for they included the Presidents of the United States and other political personages. Of the total number selected for the distinction of a small portrait, 1200 were "Americans" and 71 "immigrants." Of the 1200 "Americans," 856 were of English extraction, 129 Scotch-Irish, 57 Huguenot, 45 Scotch, 39 Dutch, 37 German, 15 Welsh, 13 Irish, 6 French, and one each of Scandinavian, Spanish, and Swiss. Of the "immigrants" 15 were English, 14 German, 11 Irish, 8 Scotch-Irish, 7 Scotch, 6 Swiss, 4 French, 3 from Spanish Provinces, and 1 each from Scandinavia, Belgium, and Poland. All the 58 whose full-page portraits are presumed to be an index to unusual prominence were found to be "Americans" and by race extraction they were distributed as follows: English 41, Scotch-Irish 8, Scotch 4, Welsh 2, Dutch, Spanish, and Irish 1 each.

Whatever may be said in objection to this index of ability (and Senator Lodge effectively answered his critics in a note appended to this study in his volume of *Historical and Political Essays*), it is apparent that a large preponderance of leadership in American politics, business, art, literature, and learning has been derived from the American stock.

This is a perfectly natural result. The founders of the Republic themselves were in large degree the children of the pick of Europe. The Puritan, Cavalier, Quaker, Scotch-Irish, Huguenot, and Dutch pioneers were not ordinary folk in any sense of the term. They were, in a measure, a race of heroes. Their sons and grandsons inherited their vigor and their striving. It is not at all singular that every President of the United States and every Chief Justice of the Federal Supreme Court has come from this stock, nor that the vast majority of Cabinet members, of distinguished Senators, of Speakers of the House, and of men of note in the House of Representatives trace back to it their lineage in whole or in part. After the middle of the nineteenth century the immigrant vote began to make itself felt, and politicians contended for the "Irish vote" and the "German vote" and later for the "Italian vote," the "Jewish vote," and the "Norwegian vote." Members of the immigrant races began to appear in Washington, and the new infusion of blood made itself felt in the political life of the country.

But, if material were available for a comprehensive analysis of American leadership in life and thought today, a larger number of names of non-native origin would no doubt appear than was disclosed in 1891 by Senator Lodge's analysis. All the learned professions, for instance, and many lines of business are finding their numbers swelled by persons of foreign parentage. This change is to be expected. The influence of environment, especially of free education and unfettered opportunity, is calling forth the talents of the children of the immigrants. The number of descendants from the American stock yearly becomes relatively less; intermarriage with the children of the foreign born is increasingly frequent. Profound changes have taken place since the American pioneers pushed their way across the Alleghanies; changes infinitely more profound have taken place even since the dawn of the twentieth century and have put to the test of Destiny the institutions which are called "American."

Nevertheless in a large sense every great tradition of the original American stock lives today: the tradition of free movement, of initiative and enterprise; the tradition of individual responsibility; the primary traditions of democracy and liberty These give a virile present meaning to the name American. A noted French journalist received this impression of a group of soldiers who in 1918 were bivouacked in his country: "I saw yesterday an American unit in which men of very varied origin abounded — French, Polish, Czech, German, English, Canadian — such their names and other facts revealed them. Nevertheless, all were of the same or similar type, a fact due apparently to the combined influences of sun, air, primary education, and environment. And one was not long in discovering that the intelligence of each and all had manifestly a wider outlook than that of the man of single racial lineage and of one country." And these men were Americans.

CHAPTER III

THE NEGRO

Not many years ago a traveler was lured into a London music hall by the sign: *Spirited American Singing and Dancing.* He saw on the stage a sextette of black-faced comedians, singing darky ragtime to the accompaniment of banjo and bones, dancing the clog and the cakewalk, and reciting negro stories with the familiar accent and smile, all to the evident delight of the audience. The man in the seat next to him remarked, "These Americans are really lively." Not only in England, but on the continent, the negro's melodies, his dialect, and his banjo, have always been identified with America. Even Americans do not at once think of the negro as a foreigner, so accustomed have they become to his presence, to his quaint mythology, his soft accent, and his genial and accommodating nature. He was to be found in every colony before the Revolution; he was an integral part of American economic life long before the great Irish and German immigrations, and, while in the mass he is confined to the South, he is found today in every State in the Union.

The negro, however, is racially the most distinctly foreign element in America. He belongs to a period of biological and racial evolution far removed from that of the white man. His habitat is the continent of the elephant and the lion, the mango and the palm, while that of the race into whose state he has been thrust is the continent of the horse and the cow, of wheat and the oak.

There is a touch of the dramatic in every phase of the negro's contact with America: his unwilling coming, his forcible detention, his final submission, his emancipation, his struggle to adapt himself to freedom, his futile competition with a superior economic order. Every step from the kidnaping, through "the voiceless woe of servitude" and the attempted redemption of his race, has been accompanied by tragedy. How else could it be when peoples of two such diverse epochs in racial evolution meet?

His coming was almost contemporaneous with that of the white man. "American slavery," says Channing,[1] "began with Columbus, possibly

[1] *History of the United States*, vol. I, p. 116.

because he was the first European who had a chance to introduce it: and negroes were brought to the New World at the suggestion of the saintly Las Casas to alleviate the lot of the unhappy and fast disappearing red man." They were first employed as body servants and were used extensively in the West Indies before their common use in the colonies on the continent. In the first plantations of Virginia a few of them were found as laborers. In 1619 what was probably the first slave ship on that coast — it was euphemistically called a "Dutch man-of-war" — landed its human cargo in Virginia. From this time onward the numbers of African slaves steadily increased. Bancroft estimated their number at 59,000 in 1714, 78,000 in 1727, and 263,000 in 1754. The census of 1790 recorded 697,624 slaves in the United States. This almost incredible increase was not due alone to the fecundity of the negro. It was due, in large measure, to the unceasing slave trade.

It is difficult to imagine more severe ordeals than the negroes endured in the day of the slave trade. Their captors in the jungles of Africa — usually neighboring tribesmen in whom the instinct for capture, enslavement, and destruction was untamed — soon learned that the aged, the inferior, the defective, were not wanted by the trader. These were usually slaughtered. Then followed for the less fortunate the long and agonizing march to the sea-board. Every one not robust enough to endure the arduous journey was allowed to perish by the way. On the coast, the agent of the trader or the middle-man awaited the captive. He was an expert at de-tecting those evidences of weakness and disease which had eluded the eye of the captor or the rigor of the march. "An African factor of fair repute," said a slave captain,[1] "is ever careful to select his human cargo with consummate prudence, so as not only to supply his employers with athletic laborers, but to avoid any taint of disease." But the severest test of all was the hideous "middle passage" which remained to every imported slave a nightmare to the day of his death. The unhappy captives were crowded into dark, unventilated holds and were fed scantily on food which was strange to their lips; they were unable to understand the tongue of their masters and often unable to understand the dia-lects of their companions in misfortune; they were depressed with their helplessness on the limitless sea, and their childish superstitions were fed by a

[1] *Captain Canot: or Twenty Years in a Slaver*, by Brantz Mayer, p. 94 ff.

thousand new terrors and emotions. It was small wonder that, when disease began its ravages in the shipload of these kidnaped beings, "the mortality of thirty per cent was not rare." That this was primarily a physical selection which made no allowance for mental aptitudes did not greatly diminish in the eyes of the master the slave's utility. The new continent needed muscle power; and so tens of thousands of able-bodied Africans were landed on American soil, alien to everything they found there.

These slaves were kidnaped from many tribes. "In our negro population," says Tillinghast, "as it came from the Western Coast of Africa, there were Wolofs and Fulans, tall, well-built, and very black, hailing from Senegambia and its vicinity; there were hundreds of thousands from the Slave Coast — Tshis, Ewes, and Yorubans, including Dahomians; and mingled with all these Soudanese negroes proper were occasional contributions of mixed stock, from the north and northeast, having an infusion of Moorish blood. There were other thousands from Lower Guinea, belonging to Bantu stock, not so black in color as the Soudanese, and thought by some to be slightly superior to them." [1] No historian has recorded these tribal differences.

[1] *The Negro in Africa and America,* p. 113.

The new environment, so strange, so ruthless, swallowed them; and, in the welter of their toil, the black men became so intermingled that all tribal distinctions soon vanished. Here and there, however, a careful observer may still find among them a man of superior mien or a woman of haughty demeanor denoting perhaps an ancestral prince or princess who once exercised authority over some African jungle village.

Slavery was soon a recognized institution in every American colony. By 1665 every colony had its slave code. In Virginia the laws became increasingly strict until the dominion of the master over his slaves was virtually absolute. In South Carolina an insurrection of slaves in 1739, which cost the lives of twenty-one whites and forty-four blacks, led to very drastic laws. Of the Northern colonies, New York seems to have been most in fear of a black peril. In 1700 there were about six thousand slaves in this colony, chiefly in the city, where there were also many free negroes, and on the large estates along the Hudson. Twice the white people of the city for reasons that have not been preserved, believing that slave insurrections were imminent, resorted to extreme and brutal measures. In 1712 they burned to death two negroes, hanged in chains a third, and condemned a fourth to be broken on the wheel. In 1741 they went so far as to burn fourteen negroes, hang eighteen, and transport seventy-one.

In New England where their numbers were relatively small and the laws were less severe, the negroes were employed chiefly in domestic service. In Quaker Pennsylvania there were many slaves, the proprietor himself being a slave owner. Ten years after the founding of Philadelphia, the authorities ordered the constables to arrest all negroes found "gadding about" on Sunday without proper permission. They were to remain in jail until Monday, receiving in lieu of meat or drink thirty-nine lashes on the bare back.

Protests against slavery were not uncommon during the colonial period; and before the Revolution was accomplished several of the States had emancipated their slaves. Vermont led the way in 1777; the Ordinance of 1787 forbade slavery in the Northwest Territory; and by 1804 all the Northern States had provided that their blacks should be set free. The opinion prevailed that slavery was on the road to gradual extinction. In the Federal Convention of 1787 this belief was crystallized into the clause making possible the prohibition of the slave trade after the year 1808. Mutual benefit organizations among the negroes, both slave and free, appeared in many States, North and South. Negro congregations were organized. The number of free negroes increased rapidly, and in the Northern States they acquired such civil rights as industry, thrift, and integrity commanded. Here and there colored persons of unusual gifts distinguished themselves in various callings and were even occasionally entertained in white households.

The industrial revolution in England, with its spinning jenny and power loom, indirectly influenced the position of the negro in America. The new machinery had an insatiable maw for cotton. It could turn such enormous quantities of raw fiber into cloth that the old rate of producing cotton was entirely inadequate. New areas had to be placed under cultivation. The South, where soil and climate combined to make an ideal cotton land, came into its own. And when Eli Whitney's gin was perfected, cotton was crowned king. Statistics tell the story: the South produced about 8000 bales of cotton in 1790; 650,000 bales in 1820; 2,469,093 bales in 1850; 5,387,052 bales in 1860.[1] This vast

[1] Coman, *Industrial History of the United States*, p. 238. Bogart gives the figures as 1,976,000 bales in 1840, and 4,675,000 bales in 1860. *Economic History of the United States*, p. 256.

increase in production called for human muscle which apparently only the negro could supply.

Once it was shown that slavery paid, its status became fixed as adamant. The South forthwith ceased weakly to apologize for it, as it had formerly done, and began to defend it, at first with some hesitation, then with boldness, and finally with vehement aggressiveness. It was economically necessary; it was morally right; it was the peculiar Southern domestic institution; and, above all, it paid. On every basis of its defense, the cotton kingdom would brook no interference from any other section of the country. So there was formed a race feudality in the Republic, rooted in profits, protected by the political power of the slave lords, and enveloped in a spirit of defiance and bitterness which reacted without mercy upon its victims. Tighter and tighter were drawn the coils of restrictions around the enslaved race. The mind and the soul as well as the body were placed under domination. They might marry to breed but not to make homes. Such charity and kindness as they experienced, they received entirely from individual humane masters; society treated them merely as chattels.

Attempted insurrections, such as that in South Carolina in 1822 and that in Virginia in 1831 in which many whites and blacks were killed, only produced harsher laws and more cruel punishments, until finally the slave became convinced that his only salvation lay in running away. The North Star was his beacon light of freedom. A few thousand made their way southward through the chain of swamps that skirt the Atlantic coast and mingled with the Indians in Florida. Tens of thousands made their way northward along well recognized routes to the free States and to Canada: the Appalachian ranges with their far-spreading spurs furnished the friendliest of these highways; the Mississippi Valley with its marshlands, forests, and swamps provided less secure hiding places; and the Cumberland Mountains, well supplied with limestone caves, offered a third pathway. At the northern end of these routes the "Underground Railway"[1] received the fugitives. From the Cumberlands, leading through the heart of Tennessee and Kentucky, this benevolent transfer stretched through Ohio and Indiana to Canada; from southern Illinois it led northward through Wisconsin; and from the Appalachian route mysterious byways led through New York and New England.

[1] See *The Anti-Slavery Crusade*, by Jesse Macy (in *The Chronicles of America*), Chapter VIII.

How many thus escaped cannot be reckoned, but it is known that the number of free negroes in the North increased so rapidly that laws discriminating against them were passed in many States. Nowhere did the negro enjoy all the rights that the white man had. In some States the free negroes were so restricted in settling as to be virtually prohibited; in others they were disfranchised; in others they were denied the right of jury duty or of testifying in court. But in spite of this discrimination on the part of the law, a great sympathy for the runaway slave spread among the people, and the fugitive carried into the heart of the North the venom of the institution of which he was the unhappy victim.

Meanwhile the slave trade responded promptly to the lure of gain which the increased demand for cotton held out. The law of 1807 prohibiting the importation of slaves had, from the date of its enactment, been virtually a dead letter. Messages of Presidents, complaints of government attorneys, of collectors and agents called attention to the continuous violation of the law; and its nullity was a matter of common knowledge. When the market price of a slave rose to $325 in 1840 and to $500 after 1850, the increase in profits made slave piracy a rather respectable business carried on by American citizens in American built ships flying the American flag and paying high returns on New York and New England capital. Owing to this steady importation there was a constant intermingling of raw stock from the jungles with the negroes who had been slaves in America for several generations.

In 1860 there were 4,441,830 negroes in the United States, of whom only 488,070 were free. About thirteen per cent of the total number were mulattoes. Among the four million slaves were men and women of every gradation of experience with civilization, from those who had just disembarked from slave ships to those whose ancestry could be traced to the earliest days of the colonies. It was not, therefore, a strictly homogeneous people upon whom were suddenly and dramatically laid the burdens and responsibilities of the freedman. Among the emancipated blacks were not a few in whom there still throbbed vigorously the savage life they had but recently left behind and who could not yet speak intelligible English. Though there were many who were skilled in household arts and in the useful customary handicrafts, large numbers were acquainted only with the simplest toil of the open fields. There were a few free blacks who possessed property, in some instances to the value of many thousands of dollars, but the great bulk were wholly inexperienced in the responsibilities of ownership. There were some who had mastered the rudiments of learning and here and there was to be found a gifted mind, but ninety per cent of the negroes were unacquainted with letters and were strangers to even the most rudimentary learning. Their religion was a picturesque blend of Christian precepts and Voodoo customs.

The Freedmen's Bureau, authorized by Congress early in 1865, had as its functions to aid the negro to develop self-control and self-reliance, to help the freedman with his new wage contracts, to befriend him when he appeared in court, and to provide for him schools and hospitals. It was a simple, slender reed for the race to lean upon until it learned to walk. But it interfered with the orthodox opinion of that day regarding individual independence and was limited to the period of war and one year thereafter. It was eyed with suspicion and was regarded with criticism by both the keepers of the *laissez faire* faith and the former slave owners. It established a number of schools and made a modest beginning in peasant proprietorship and free labor.[1]

[1] See *The Sequel of Appomattox*, by Walter L. Fleming (in *The Chronicles of America*), Chapter IV.

When this temporary guide was withdrawn, private organizations to some extent took its place. The American Missionary Association continued the educational work, and volunteers shouldered other benevolences. But no power and no organization could take the place of the national authority. If the Freedmen's Bureau could have been stripped of those evil-intentioned persons who used it for private gain, been so organized as to enlist the support of the Southern white population, and been continued until a new generation of blacks were prepared for civil life, the colossal blunders and criminal misfits of that bitter period of transition might have been avoided. But political opportunism spurned comprehensive plans, and the negro suddenly found himself forced into social, political, and economic competition with the white man.

The social and political struggle that followed was short-lived. There were a few desperate years under the domination of the carpetbagger and the Ku Klux Klan, a period of physical coercion and intimidation. Within a decade the negro vote was uncast or uncounted, and the grandfather clauses soon completed the political mastery of the former slave owner. A strict interpretation of the

Civil Rights Act denied the application of the equality clause of the Constitution to social equality, and the social as well as the political separation of the two stocks was also accomplished. "Jim Crow," cars, separate accommodations in depots and theaters, separate schools, separate churches, attempted segregations in cities — these are all symbolic of two separate races forcibly united by constitutional amendments.

But the economic struggle continued, for the black man, even if politically emasculated and socially isolated, had somehow to earn a living. In their first reaction of anger and chagrin, some of the whites here and there made attempts to reduce freedmen to their former servitude, but their efforts were effectually checked by the Fifteenth Amendment. An ingenious peonage, however, was created by means of the criminal law. Strict statutes were passed by States on guardianship, vagrancy, and petty crimes. It was not difficult to bring charges under these statutes, and the heavy penalties attached, together with the wide discretion permitted to judge and jury, made it easy to subject the culprit to virtual serfdom for a term of years. He would be leased to some contractor, who would pay for his keep and would profit by his toil. Whatever justification there may have been for these statutes, the convict lease system soon fell into disrepute, and it has been generally abandoned.

It was upon the land that the freedman naturally sought his economic salvation. He was experienced in cotton growing. But he had neither acres nor capital. These he had to find and turn to his own uses ere he could really be economically free. So he began as a farm laborer, passed through various stages of tenantry, and finally graduated into land ownership. One finds today examples of every stage of this evolution.[1] There is first the farm laborer, receiving at the end of the year a fixed wage. He is often supplied with house and garden and usually with food and clothing. There are many variations of this labor contract. The "cropper" is barely a step advanced above the laborer, for he, too, furnishes nothing but labor, while the landlord supplies house, tools, live stock, and seed. His wage, however, is paid not in cash but in a stipulated share of the crop. From this share he must pay for the supplies received and interest thereon. This method, however, has proved to be a mutually unsatisfactory arrangement

[1] See *The New South* by Holland Thompson (in *The Chronicles of America*), Chapters IV and VII.

and is usually limited to hard pressed owners of poor land.

The larger number of the negro farmers are tenants on shares or metayers. They work the land on their own responsibility, and this degree of independence appeals to them. They pay a stipulated portion of the crop as rent. If they possess some capital and the rental is fair, this arrangement proves satisfactory. But as very few negro metayers possess the needed capital, they resort to a system of crop-lienage under which a local retail merchant advances the necessary supplies and obtains a mortgage on the prospective crop. Many negro farmers, however, have achieved the independence of cash renters, assuming complete control of their crops and the disposition of their time. And finally, 241,000 negro farmers are landowners.[1] By 1910 nearly 900,000 negroes had achieved some degree of rural economic stability.

The negro has not been so fortunate in his attempts to make a place for himself in the industrial world. The drift to the cities began soon after emancipation. During the first decade, the dissatisfaction with the landlordism which then prevailed, seconded by the demand for unskilled labor

[1] *Negroes in the United States*, Census Bulletin No. 129, p. 37.

in the rapidly growing cities, drew the negroes from the land in such considerable numbers that the landowners were induced to make more liberal terms to keep the laborers on their farms. While there has been a large increase in the number of negroes engaged in agriculture, there has at the same time been a very marked current from the smaller communities to the new industrial cities of the South and to some of the manufacturing centers of the North. In recent years there have been whole-sale importations of negro laborers into many Northern cities and towns, sometimes as strike breakers but more frequently to supply the urgent demand for unskilled labor. Many of the smaller manufacturing towns of New York, Ohio, Pennsylvania, Illinois, and Indiana are accumulating a negro population.

Very few of these industrial negroes, however, are skilled workers. They toil rather as ordinary day laborers, porters, stevedores, teamsters, and domestics. There has been a great deal written of the decline of the negro artisan. Walter F. Willcox, the eminent statistician, after a careful study of the facts concludes that economically "the negro as a race is losing ground, is being confined more and more to the inferior and less remunerative occupations, and is not sharing proportionately to his numbers in the prosperity of the country as a whole or of the section in which he mainly lives."

It appears, therefore, that the pathway of emancipation has not led the negro out of the ranks of humble toil and into racial equality. In order to equip him more effectively for a place in the world, industrial schools have been established, among which the most noted is the Tuskegee Institute. Its founder, Booker T. Washington, advised his fellow negroes to yield quietly to the political and social distinctions raised against them and to perfect themselves in handicrafts and the mechanic arts, in the faith that civil rights would ultimately follow economic power and recognized industrial capacity. His teaching received the almost unanimous approval of both North and South. But opinion among his own people was divided, and in 1905 the "Niagara Movement" was launched, followed five years later by the organizing of the National Association for the Advancement of Colored People. This organization advised a more aggressive attitude towards race distinctions, outspokenly advocated race equality, demanded the negro's rights, and maintained a restless propaganda. These champions of the race possibilities of the negro point to the material advance made since slavery; to the 500,000 houses and the 221,000 farms owned by them; their 22,000 small retail businesses and their 40 banks; to the 40,000 churches with nearly 4,000,000 members; to the 200 colleges and secondary schools maintained for negroes and largely supported by them; to their 100 old people's homes, 30 hospitals, 300 periodicals; to the 6000 physicians, dentists, and nurses; the 30,000 teachers, the 18,000 clergymen. They point to the beacon lights of their genius: Frederick Douglass, statesman; J. C. Price, orator; Booker T. Washington, educator; W. E. B. DuBois, scholar; Paul Laurence Dunbar, poet; Charles W. Chestnutt, novelist. And they compare this record of 50 years' achievement with the preceding 245 years of slavery.

This, however, is only one side of the shield. There is another side, nowhere better illustrated, perhaps, than in the neglected negro gardens of the South. Near every negro hut is a garden patch large enough to supply the family with vegetables for the entire year, but it usually is neglected. "If they have any garden at all," says a negro critic from Tuskegee, "it is apt to be choked with weeds and other noxious growths. With every advantage of soil and climate and with a steady market if they live near any city or large town, few of the colored farmers get any benefit from this, one of the most profitable of all industries." In marked contrast to these wild and unkempt patches are the gardens of the Italians who have recently invaded portions of the South and whose garden patches are almost miraculously productive. And this invasion brings a real threat to the future of the negro. His happy-go-lucky ways, his easy philosophy of life, the remarkable ease with which he severs home ties and shifts from place to place, his indifference to property obligations — these negative defects in his character may easily lead to his economic doom if the vigorous peasantry of Italy and other lands are brought into competition with him.

CHAPTER IV

AMERICA has long been a gigantic Utopia. To every immigrant since the founding of Jamestown this coast has gleamed upon the horizon as a Promised Land. America, too, has provided convenient plots of ground, as laboratories for all sorts of vagaries, where, unhampered by restrictions and unannoyed by inquisitive neighbors, enthusiastic dreamers could attempt to reconstruct society. Whenever an eccentric in Europe conceived a social panacea no matter how absurd, he said, "Let's go to America and try it out." There were so many of these enterprises that their exact number is unknown. Many of them perished in so brief a time that no friendly chronicler has even saved their names from oblivion. But others lived, some for a year, some for a decade, and few for more than a generation. They are of interest today not only because they brought a considerable number of foreigners to America, but also because in their history may be observed many of the principles of communism, or socialism, at work under favorable conditions. While the theory of Marxian socialism differs in certain details from these communistic experiments, the foreign-made nostrums so brazenly proclaimed today wherever malcontents are gathered together is in essence nothing new in America. Communism was tried and found wanting by the Pilgrim Fathers; since then it has been tried and found wanting over and over again. Some of the communistic colonies, it will appear, waxed fat out of the resources of their lands; but, in the end, even those which were most fortunate and successful withered away, and their remnants were absorbed by the great competitive life that surrounded them.

There were two general types of these communities, the sectarian and the economic. Frequently they combined a peculiar religious belief with the economic practice of having everything in common. The sectarians professed to be neither proselyters nor propagandists but religious devotees, accepting communism as a physical advantage as well as a spiritual balm, and seeking in seclusion and quiet merely to save their own souls.

The majority of the religious communists came from Germany — the home, also, of Marxian socialism in later years — where persecution was the lot of innumerable little sects which budded after the Reformation. They came usually as whole colonies, bringing both leaders and membership with them.[1] Probably the earliest to arrive in America were the Labadists, who denied the doctrine of original sin, discarded the Sabbath, and held strict views of marriage. In 1684, under the leadership of Peter Sluyter or Schluter (an assumed name, his original name being Vorstmann), some of these Labadists settled on the Bohemia River in Delaware. They were sent out from the mother colony in West Friesland to select a site for the entire body, but it does not appear that any others migrated, for within fifteen years the American

---

[1] As is usual among people who pride themselves on their peculiarities there were variations of opinion among these sects which led to schisms. The Mennonites contained at one time no less than eleven distinct branches, among them the Amish, Old and New, whose ridiculous singularity of dress, in which they discarded all ornaments and even buttons, earned them the nickname "Hooks and Eyes." But no matter how aloof these sects held themselves from the world, or what asceticism they practiced upon themselves, or what spiritual and economic fraternity they displayed to each other, they possessed a remarkable native cunning in bargaining over a bushel of wheat or a shoat, and for a time most of their communities prospered.

colony was reduced to eight men. Sluyter evidently had considerable business capacity, for he became a wealthy tobacco planter and slave trader.

In 1693 Johann Jacob Zimmermann, a distinguished mathematician and astronomer and the founder of an order of mystics called Pietists, started for America, to await the coming of the millennium, which his calculations placed in the autumn of 1694. But the fate of common mortals overtook the unfortunate leader and he died just as he was ready to sail from Rotterdam. About forty members of his brotherhood settled in the forests on the heights near Germantown, Pennsylvania, and, under the guidance of Johann Kelpius, achieved a unique influence over the German peasantry in that vicinity. The members of the brotherhood made themselves useful as teachers and in various handicrafts. They were especially in demand among the superstitious for their skill in casting horoscopes, using divining rods, and carving potent amulets. Their mysterious astronomical tower on the heights of the Wissahickon was the Mecca of the curious and the distressed. To the gentle Kelpius was ascribed the power of healing, but he was himself the victim of consumption. The brotherhood did not long survive his death in 1708 or 1709. Their astrological instruments may now be seen in the collections of the Pennsylvania Philosophical Society.

The first group of Dunkards (a name derived from their method of baptism, *eintunken*, to immerse) settled in Pennsylvania in 1719. A few years later they were joined by Conrad Beissel (Beizel or Peysel). This man had come to America to unite with the Pietist group in Germantown, but, as Kelpius was dead and his followers dispersed he joined the Dunkards. His desires for a monastic life drove him into solitary meditation — tradition says he took shelter in a cave — where he came to the conviction that the seventh day of the week should be observed as the day of rest. This conclusion led to friction with the Dunkards; and as a result, with three men and two women, Beissel founded in 1728 on the Cocalico River, the cloister of Ephrata. From this arose the first communistic Eden successfully established in America and one of the few to survive to the present century. Though in 1900 the community numbered only seventeen members, in its prime while Beissel was yet alive it sheltered three hundred, owned a prosperous paper mill, a grist mill, an oil mill, a fulling mill, a printing press, a schoolhouse, dwellings for the married members, and large dormitories for the celibates. The meeting-house was built entirely without metal, following literally the precedent of Solomon, who built his temple "so that there was neither hammer nor ax nor any tool of iron heard in the house while it was building." Wooden pegs took the place of nails, and the laths were fastened laboriously into grooves. Averse to riches, Beissel's people refused gifts from William Penn, King George III, and other prominent personages. The pious Beissel was a very capable leader, with a passion for music and an ardor for simplicity. He instituted among the unmarried members of the community a celibate order embracing both sexes, and he reduced the communal life of both the religious and secular members to a routine of piety and labor. The society was known, even in England, for the excellence of its paper, for the good workmanship of its printing press, and especially for the quality of its music, which was composed largely by Beissel. His chorals were among the first composed and sung in America. His school, too, was of such quality that it drew pupils from Baltimore and Philadelphia. After his death in 1786, in his seventy-second year, his successor tried for twenty-eight years to maintain the discipline and distinction of the order. It was eventually deemed prudent to incorporate the society under the laws of the State and to entrust its management to a board of trustees, and the cloistered life of the community became a memory.

A community patterned after Ephrata was founded in 1800 by Peter Lehman at Snow Hill, in Franklin County, Pennsylvania. It consisted of some forty German men and women living in cloisters but relieving the monotony of their toil and the rigor of their piety with music. As in Ephrata, there was a twofold membership, the consecrated and the secular. The entire community, however, vanished after the death of its founder.

When Beissel's Ephrata was in its heyday, the Moravians, under the patronage of Count Zinzendorf of Saxony, established in 1741 a community on the Lehigh River in Pennsylvania, named Bethlehem in token of their humility. The colony provided living and working quarters for both the married and unmarried members. After about twenty years of experimenting, the communistic regimen was abandoned. Bethlehem, however, continued to thrive, and its schools and its music became widely known.

The story of the Harmonists, one of the most successful of all the communistic colonies is even more interesting. The founder, Johann Georg Rapp, had been a weaver and vine gardener in the little village of Iptingen in Württemberg. He drew upon himself and his followers the displeasure of the Church by teaching that religion was a personal matter between the individual and his God; that the Bible, not the pronouncements of the clergy, should be the guide to the true faith, and that the ordinances of the Church were not necessarily the ordinances of God. The petty persecutions which these doctrines brought upon him and his fellow separatists turned them towards liberal America. In 1803 Rapp and some of his companions crossed the sea and selected as a site for their colony five thousand acres of land in Butler County, Pennsylvania. There they built the new town of Harmony, to which came about six hundred persons, all told. On February 15, 1805 they organized the Harmony Society and signed a solemn agreement to merge all their possessions in one common lot.[1] Among

---

[1] Under the communal contract, which was later upheld by the Supreme Court of the United States, members agreed to merge their properties and to renounce all claims for services; and the community, on its part, agreed to support the members and to repay without interest, to any one desiring to withdraw, the amount he had put into the common fund.

them were a few persons of education and property, but most of them were sturdy, thrifty mechanics and peasants, who, under the skillful direction of Father Rapp, soon transformed the forest into a thriving community. After a soul stirring revival in 1807, they adopted celibacy. Those who were married did not separate but lived together in solemn self-restraint, "treating each other as brother and sister in Christ." [1] Their belief that the second coming of the Lord was imminent no doubt strengthened their resolution. At this time, also, the men all agreed to forego the use of tobacco — no small sacrifice on the part of hard-working laborers.

The region, however, was unfavorable to the growth of the grape, which was the favorite Württemberg crop. In 1814 the society accordingly sold the communal property for $100,000 and removed to a site on the Wabash River, in Indiana, where, under the magic of their industry, the beautiful village of New Harmony arose in one year, and where many of their sturdy buildings still remain a testimony to their honest craftsmanship. Unfortunately, however, two pests appeared which they had not foreseen. Harassed by malaria and

[1] *Communistic Societies of the United States*, by Charles Nordhoff, p. 73.

meddlesome neighbors, Father Rapp a third time sought a new Canaan. In 1825 he sold the entire site to Robert Owen, the British philanthropic socialist, and the Harmonists moved back to Pennsylvania. They built their third and last home on the Ohio, about twenty miles from Pittsburgh, and called it Economy in prophetic token of the wealth which their industry and shrewdness would soon bring in.

The chaste and simple beauty of this village was due to the skill and good taste of Friedrich Reichert Rapp, an architect and stone cutter, the adopted son of Father Rapp. The fine proportions of the plain buildings, with their vines festooned between the upper and lower windows, the quaint and charming gardens, the tantalizing labyrinth where visitors lost themselves in an attempt to reach the Summer House — these were all of his creation. Friedrich Rapp was also a poet, an artist, and a musician. He gathered a worthy collection of paintings and a museum of Indian relics and objects of natural history. He composed many of the fine hymns which impress every visitor to Economy. He was likewise an energetic and skillful business man and represented the colony in its external affairs until his death in 1834. He was elected a member of the convention that framed the first constitution of Indiana, and later he was made a member of the legislature. Father Rapp, who possessed rare talents as an organizer, controlled the internal affairs of the colony. Those who left the community because unwilling to abide its discipline often pronounced their leader a narrow autocrat. But there can be no doubt that eminent good sense and gentleness tempered his judgments. He personally led the community in industry, in prayers, and in faith, until 1847, when death removed him. A council of nine elders elected by the members was then charged with the spiritual guidance of the community, and two trustees were appointed to administer its business affairs.

Economy was a German community where German was spoken and German customs were maintained, although every one also spoke English. As there were but few accessions to the community and from time to time there were defections and withdrawals, the membership steadily declined[1];

[1] The largest membership was attained in 1827, when 522 were enrolled. There were 391 in 1836; 321 in 1846; 170 in 1864; 146 in 1866; 70 in 1879; 34 in 1888; 37 in 1892; 10 in 1897; 8 in 1902, only two of whom were men; and in 1903, three women and one man. The population of Economy, however, was always much larger than the communal membership.

but while the community was dwindling in membership it was rapidly increasing in wealth. Oil and coal were found on some of its lands; the products of its mills and looms, of its wine presses and distilleries, were widely and favorably known; and its outside investments, chiefly in manufactories and railroads, yielded even greater returns. These outside interests, indeed, became in time the sole support of the community for, as the membership fell away, the local industries had to be shut down. Then it was that communistic methods of doing business became inadequate and the colony ran into difficulties. An expert accountant in 1892 disclosed the debts of the community to be about one and a half million dollars. But the outside industrial enterprises in which the community had invested were sound; and the vast debt was paid. The society remained solvent, with a huge surplus, though out of prosperity not of its own making. When the lands at Economy were eventually sold, about eight acres were reserved to the few survivors of the society, including the Great House of Father Rapp and its attractive garden, with the use of the church and dwellings, so that they might spend their last days in the peaceful surroundings that had brought them prosperity and happiness.

Lead me, Father, out of harm
To the quiet Zoar farm
If it be Thy will.

So sang another group of simple German separatists, of whom some three hundred came to America
from Württemberg in 1817, under the leadership of
Joseph Bimeler (Bäumeler) and built the village
of Zoar in Tuscarawas County, Ohio. They acquired five thousand acres of land and signed ar-
ticles of association in April, 1819, turning all their
individual property and all their future earnings
into a common fund to be managed by an elected
board of directors. The community provided its
members with their daily necessities and two suits
of clothes a year. The members were assigned to
various trades which absorbed all their time and
left them very little strength for amusement or
reading. Their one recreation was singing. The
society was bound to celibacy until the marriage
of Bimeler to his housekeeper; thereafter marriage
was permitted but not encouraged.

In 1832 the society was incorporated under the
laws of Ohio, and until its dissolution it was managed as a corporation. A few Germans joined the
society. No American ever requested admission.
Joseph Bimeler was elected Agent General and

thereby became the chosen as well as the natural leader of the community. Like other patriarchs of that epoch who led their following into the wilderness, he was a man of some education and many gifts. He was the spiritual mentor; but his piety, which was sincere and simple, did not rob him of the shrewdness necessary to material success. His followers were loyally devoted to him. They built for him the largest house in the community, a fine colonial manor house, where he dwelt in comparative luxury and reigned as their "King." When he died in 1853 he had seen the prosperity of his colony reach its zenith. It remained small. Scarcely more than three hundred members ever dwelt in the village which, in spite of its profusion of vines and flowers, lacked the informal quaintness and originality of Rapp's Economy. The Tuscarawas River furnished power for their flour mill, whose products were widely sought. There was also a woolen mill, a planing mill, a foundry, and a machine shop. The beer made by the community was famous all the country round, and for a time its pottery and tile works turned out interesting and quaint products. But one by one these small industries succumbed to the competition of the greater world. At last even an alien brew supplanted the good local beer. When the railroad tapped the village, and it was incorporated (1884) and assumed an official worldliness with its mayor and councilmen, it lost its isolation, summer visitors flocked in, and a "calaboose" was needed for the benefit of the sojourners!

The third generation was now grown. A number of dissatisfied members had left. Many of the children never joined the society but found work elsewhere. A great deal of the work had to be done by hired help. Under the leadership of the younger element it was decided in 1898 to abandon communism. Appraisers and surveyors were set to work to parcel out the property. Each of the 136 members received a cash dividend, a home in the village, and a plot of land. The average value of each share, which was in the neighborhood of $1500, was not a large return for three generations of communistic experimentation. But these had been, after all, years of moderate competence and quiet contentment, and if they took their toll in the coin of hope, as their song set forth, then these simple Württembergers were fully paid.

The Inspirationists were a sect that made many converts in Germany, Holland, and Switzerland in the eighteenth century. They believed in direct revelations from God through chosen "instruments." In 1817, a new leader appeared among them in the person of Christian Metz, a man of great personal charm, worldly shrewdness, and spiritual fervor. Allied with him was Barbara Heynemann, a simple maid without education, who learned to read the Scriptures after she was twenty-three years of age. Endowed with the peculiar gift of "translation," she was cherished by the sect as an instrument of God for revealing His will.

To this pair came an inspiration to lead their harassed followers to America. In 1842 they purchased the Seneca Indian Reservation near Buffalo, New York. They called their new home Ebenezer, and in 1843 they organized the Ebenezer Society, under a constitution which pledged them to communism. Over eight hundred peasants and artisans joined the colony, and their industry soon had created a cluster of five villages with mills, workshops, schools, and dwellings. But they were continually annoyed by the Indians from whom they had purchased the site and were distracted by the rapidly growing city of Buffalo, which was only five miles away!

This threat of worldliness brought a revelation that they must seek greater seclusion. A large tract on the Iowa River was purchased, and to this new site the population was gradually transferred. There they built Amana. Within a radius of six miles, five subsidiary villages sprang up, each one laid out like a German *dorf*, with its cluster of shops and mills, and the cottages scattered informally on the main road. When the railway tapped the neighborhood, the community in self-defense purchased the town that contained the railway station. So when the good Christian Metz died in 1867, at the age of seventy-two, his pious followers, thanks to his sagacity, were possessed of some twenty-six thousand acres of rich Iowa land and seven thriving villages, comfortably housing about 1400 of the faithful. Barbara Heynemann died in 1883, and since her death no "instrument" has been found to disclose the will of God. But many ponderous tomes of "revelations" have survived and these are faithfully read and their naïve personal directions and inhibitions are still generally obeyed. The Bible, however, remains the main guide of these people, and they follow its instructions with childish literalism. Until quite recently they clung to the simple dress and the austere life of their earlier years. The solidarity of the community has been maintained with rare skill. The "Great Council of the Brethren" upon whom is laid the burden of directing all the affairs, has avoided government by mass meeting, discouraged irresponsible talk and criticism, and, as an aristocracy of elders, has shrewdly controlled the material and spiritual life of the community.

The society has received many new members. There have been accessions from Zoar and Economy and one or two Americans have joined. The "Great Council," in its desire to maintain the homogeneity of the group, rejects the large number of applications for membership received every year. Over sixty per cent of the young people who have left the community to try the world have come back to "colony trousers" or "colony skirts," symbols of the complete submergence of the individual.

Celibacy has been encouraged but never enjoined, and the young people are permitted to marry, if the Spirit gives its sanction, the Elders their consent, and if the man has reached the age of twenty-four years. The two sexes are rigidly separated in school, in church, at work, and in the communal dining rooms. Each family lives in a house, but there are communal kitchens, where meals are served to groups of twenty or more.

Every member receives an annual cash bonus varying from $25 to $75 and a pass book to record his credits at the "store." The work is doled out among the members, who take pride in the quality rather than in the quantity of their product. All forms of amusement are forbidden; music, which flourished in other German communities, is suppressed; and even reading for pleasure or information was until recently under the ban.

The only symbols of gayety in the villages are the flowers, and these are everywhere in lavish abundance, softening the austere lines of the plain and unpainted houses. No architect has been allowed to show his skill, no artist his genius, in the shaping of this rigorous life. But its industries flourish. Amana calico and Amana woolens are known in many markets. The livestock is of the finest breeds; the products of the fields and orchards are the choicest. But the modern visitor wonders how long this prosperity will be able to maintain that isolation which alone insured the communal solidarity. Already store clothes are being worn, photographs are seen on the walls, "worldly" furniture is being used, libraries, those openers of closed minds, are in every schoolhouse, and newspapers and magazines are "allowed."

The experiences of Eric Janson and his devotees whom he led out of Sweden to Bishop Hill Colony, in Illinois, are replete with dramatic and tragic details. Janson was a rugged Swedish peasant, whose eloquence and gift of second sight made him the prophet of the Devotionalists, a sect that attempted to reëstablish the simplicity of the primitive church among the Lutherans of Scandinavia. Driven from pillar to post by the relentless hatred of the Established Church, they sought refuge in America, where Janson planned a theocratic socialistic community. Its communism was based entirely upon religious convictions, for neither Janson nor any of his illiterate followers had heard of the politico-economic systems of French reformers. Over one thousand young and vigorous peasants followed him to America. The first contingent of four hundred arrived in 1846 and spent their first winter in untold miseries and privations, with barely sufficient food, but with enough spiritual fervor to kindle two religious services a day and three on Sunday. Attacking the vast prairies with their primitive implements, harvesting grain with the sickle and grinding it by hand when their water power gave out, sheltering themselves in tents and caves, enduring agues and fevers, hunger and cold, the majority still remained loyal to the leader whose eloquence fired them with a sustaining hope. Thrift, unremitting toil, the wonderful fertility of the prairie, the high price of wheat, flax, and broom corn, were bound to bring prosperity. In 1848 they built a huge brick dormitory and dining hall, a great frame church, and a number of smaller dwellings. Improved housing at once told on the general health, though in the next year a scourge of cholera, introduced by some newcomer, claimed 143 members.

In the meantime John Root, an adventurer from Stockholm, who had served in the American army, arrived at the colony and soon fell in love with the cousin of Eric Janson. The prophet gave his consent to the marriage on condition that, if at any time Root wished to leave the colony, his wife should be permitted to remain if she desired. A written agreement acknowledged Root's consent to these conditions. He soon tired of a life for which he had not the remotest liking, and, failing to entice his wife away with him, he kidnaped her and forcibly detained her in Chicago, whence she was rescued by a valiant band of the colonists. In retaliation the irate husband organized a mob of frontiers folk to drive out the fanatics as they had a

short time before driven out Brigham Young and
his Mormons. But the neighbors of the colonists,
having learned their sterling worth, came to the
rescue. Root then began legal proceedings against
Janson. In May, 1850, while in court the rene-
gade deliberately shot and killed the prophet. The
community in despair awaited three days the return to life of the man whom they looked upon as
a representative of Christ sent to earth to rebuild
the Tabernacle.

Janson had been a very poor manager, however, and the colony was in debt. In order quickly to obtain money, he had sent Jonas Olsen, the
ablest and strongest of his followers, to California to seek gold to wipe out the debt. Upon hear-
ing of the tragedy, Olsen hastened back to Bishop Hill and was soon in charge of affairs. In
1853 he obtained for the colony a charter of in-
corporation which vested the entire management
of the property in seven trustees. These men,
under the by-laws adopted, became also the spiritual mentors, and the colonists, unacquainted with
democratic usages in government, submitted willingly to the leadership of this oligarchy. A new era
of great material prosperity now set in. The village was rebuilt. The great house was enlarged so

that all the inhabitants could be accommodated in its vast communal dining room. Trees were planted along the streets. Shops and mills were erected, and a hotel became the means of introducing strangers to the community.

Meanwhile Olsen was growing more and more arbitrary and, after a bitter controversy, he imposed celibacy upon the members. This was the beginning of the end. One of the trustees, Olaf Jansen, a good-natured peasant who could not keep his accounts but who had a peasant's sagacity for a bargain, wormed his way into financial control. He wanted to make the colony rich, but he led it to the verge of bankruptcy. He became a speculator and promoter. Stories of his shortcomings were whispered about and in 1860 the peasant colony revolted and deposed Olaf from office. He then had himself appointed receiver to wind up the corporation's affairs, and in the following year the communal property was distributed. Every member, male and female, thirty-five years of age received a full share which "consisted of 22 acres of land, one timber lot of nearly 2 acres, one town lot, and an equal part of all barns, houses, cattle, hogs, sheep or other domestic animals and all farming implements and household utensils." Those under thirty-five received according to their age. Had these shares been unencumbered, this would have represented a fair return for their labor. But Olaf had made no half-way business of his financial ambitions, and the former members who now were melting peacefully and rather contentedly into the general American life found themselves saddled with his obligations. The "colony case" became famous among Illinois lawyers and dragged through twelve years of litigation. Thus the glowing fraternal communism of poor Janson ended in the drab discord of an American lawsuit.

In 1862 the followers of Jacob Hutter, a Mennonite martyr who was burned at the stake in Innsbruck in the sixteenth century, founded the Old Elmspring Community on the James River in South Dakota. During the Thirty Years' War these saintly Quaker-like German folk had found refuge in Moravia, whence they had been driven into Hungary, later into Rumania, and then into Russia. As their objection to military service brought them into conflict with the Czar's government, they finally determined to migrate to America. In 1874 they had all reached South Dakota, where they now live in five small communities. Scarcely four hundred all told,

they cling to their ancient ambition to keep themselves "unspotted from the world," and so have
evolved a self-sustaining communal life, characterized by great simplicity of dress, of speech,
and of living. They speak German and refrain
entirely from voting and from other political activity. They are farmers and practise only those
handicrafts which are necessary to their own communal welfare.

While most of these German sectarian communities had only a slight economic effect upon the
United States, their influence upon immigration has
been extensive. In the early part of the last century, it was difficult to obtain authentic news concerning America in the remote hamlets of Europe.
All sorts of vague and grotesque notions about this
country were afloat. Every member of these communities, when he wrote to those left behind, became a living witness of the golden opportunities
offered in the new land. And, unquestionably, a
considerable share of the great German influx in
the middle of the nineteenth century can be traced
to the dissemination of knowledge by this means.
Mikkelsen says of the Jansonists that their "letters
home concerning the new country paved the way
for that mighty tide of Swedish immigration which

in a few years began to roll in upon Illinois and the Northwest."

The Shakers are the oldest and the largest communistic sect to find a congenial home in America. The cult originated in Manchester, England, with Ann Lee, a "Shaking Quaker," who never learned to read or write but depended upon revelation for doctrine and guidance. "By a direct revelation," says the Shaker Compendium, she was "instructed to come to America." Obedient to the vision, she sailed from Liverpool in the summer of 1774, accompanied by six men and two women, among whom were her husband, a brother, and a niece. This little flock settled in the forests near Albany, New York. Abandoned by her husband, the prophetess went from place to place, proclaiming her peculiar doctrines. Soon she became known as "Mother Ann" and was reputed to have supernatural powers. At the time of her death in 1784 she had numerous followers in western New England and eastern New York.

In 1787 they founded their first Shaker community at Mount Lebanon. Within a few years other societies were organized in New York, Massachusetts, New Hampshire, Maine, and Connecticut. On the wave of the great religious revival at the

beginning of the nineteenth century their doctrines were carried west. The cult achieved its
highest prosperity in the decade following 1830,
when it numbered eighteen societies and about six
thousand members.

In shrewd and capable hands, the sect soon had
both an elaborate system of theology based upon
the teachings of Mother Ann and also an effective organization. The communal life, ordaining
celibacy, based on industry, and constructed in
the strictest economy, achieved material prosperity and evidently brought spiritual consolation to
those who committed themselves to its isolation.
Although originating in England, the sect is confined wholly to America and has from the first recruited its membership almost wholly from native
Americans.

Another of these social experiments was the Oneida Community and its several ephemeral branches.
Though it was of American origin and the members
were almost wholly American, it deserves passing
mention. The founder, John Humphrey Noyes, a
graduate of Dartmouth and a Yale divinity student,
conceived a system of communal life which should
make it possible for the individual to live without
sin. This perfectionism, he believed, necessitated

the abolition of private property through communism, the abolition of sickness through complete coöperation of the individual with God, and the abolition of the family through a "scientific" coöperation of the sexes. The Oneida Community was financially very prosperous. Its "stirpiculture," Noyes's high-sounding synonym for free love, brought it, however, into violent conflict with public opinion, and in 1879 "complex marriages" gave way to monogamous families. In the following year the communistic holding of property gave way to a joint stock company, under whose skillful management the prosperity of the community continues today.

The American Utopias based upon an assumed economic altruism were much more numerous than those founded primarily upon religion but, as they were recruited almost wholly from Americans, they need engage our attention only briefly. There were two groups of economic communistic experiments, similar in their general characteristics but differing in their origin. One took its inspiration directly from Robert Owen, the distinguished philanthropist and successful cotton manufacturer of Scotland; the other from Fourier, the noted French social philosopher.

In 1825 Robert Owen purchased New Harmony, Rapp's village in Indiana and its thirty thousand appurtenant acres. When Owen came to America he was already famous. Great throngs flocked to hear this practical man utter the most visionary sentiments. At Washington, for instance, he lectured to an auditory that included great senators and famous representatives, members of the Supreme Court and of the Cabinet, President Monroe and Adams, the President-elect. He displayed to his eager hearers the plans and specifications of the new human order, his glorified apartment house with all the external paraphernalia of selective human perfection drawn to scale.

For a brief period New Harmony was the communistic capital of the world. It was discussed everywhere and became, says its chronicler, "the rendezvous of the enlightened and progressive people from all over the United States and northern Europe." It achieved a sort of motley cosmopolitanism. A "Boat Load of Knowledge" carried from Pittsburgh the most distinguished group of scientists that had hitherto been brought together in America. It included William Maclure, a Scotchman who came to America, at the age of thirty three, ambitious to make a geological survey of the country and whose learning and energy soon earned him the title of "Father of American Geology"; Thomas Say, "the Father of American Zoölogy"; Charles Alexander Lesueur, a distinguished naturalist from the *Jardin des Plantes* of Paris; Constantine S. Rafinesque, a scientific nomad whose studies of fishes took him everywhere and whose restless spirit forbade him remaining long anywhere; Gerard Troost, a Dutch scientist who later did pioneer work in western geology; Joseph Neef, a well-known Pestalozzian educator, together with two French experts in that system; and Owen's four brilliant sons. A few artists and musicians and all sorts of reformers, including Fanny Wright, an ardent and very advanced suffragette, joined these scientists in the new Eden. Owen had issued a universal invitation to the "industrious and well disposed," but his project offered also the lure of a free meal ticket for the improvident and the glitter of novelty for the restless.

"I am come to this country," Owen said in his opening words at New Harmony, "to introduce an entire new state of society, to change it from the ignorant, selfish system to an enlightened social system, which shall gradually unite all interests into one, and remove all causes for contests between individuals."[1] But the germs of dissolution were already present in the extreme individuality of the members of this new society. Here was no homogeneous horde of docile German peasants waiting to be commanded. What Father Rapp could do, Owen could not. The sifting process had begun too late. Seven different constitutions issued in rapid succession attempted in vain to discover a common bond of action. In less than two years Owen's money was gone, and nine hundred or more disillusioned persons rejoined the more individualistic world. Many of them subsequently achieved distinction in professional and public callings. Owen's widely advertised experiment was fecund, however, and produced some eleven other short-lived communistic attempts, of which the most noted were at Franklin, Haverstraw, and Coxsackie in New York, Yellow Springs and Kendal in Ohio, and Forestville and Macluria in Indiana.

Fourierism found its principal apostle in this country in Arthur Brisbane, whose *Social Destiny of Man*, published in 1840, brought to America the French philosopher's naïve, social regimen of

[1] *The New Harmony Movement* by G. B. Lockwood, p. 83.

reducing the world of men to simple units called phalanxes, whose barrack-like routine should insure plenty, equality, and happiness. Horace Greeley, with characteristic, erratic eagerness, pounced upon the new gospel, and Brisbane obtained at once a wide circle of sympathetic readers through the *Tribune*. Thirty-four phalanxes were organized in a short time, most of them with an incredible lack of foresight. They usually lasted until the first payment on the mortgage was due, though a few weathered the buffetings of fortune for several years. Brook Farm in Massachusetts and the Wisconsin phalanx each endured six years, and the North American phalanx at Red Bank, New Jersey, lasted thirteen years.

Icaria is a romantic sequel to the Owen and Fourier colonies. It antedated Brisbane's revival of Fourierism, was encouraged by Owenism, survived both, and formed a living link between the utopianism of the early nineteenth century and the utilitarian socialism of the twentieth. Étienne Cabet was one of those interesting Frenchmen whose fertile minds and instinct for rapid action made France during the nineteenth century kaleidoscopic with social and political events. Though educated for the bar, Cabet devoted

himself to social and political reform. As a young
man he was a director in that powerful secret order,
the Carbonari, and was elected to the French cham-
ber of deputies, but his violent attitude toward the
Government was such that in 1834 he was obliged
to flee to London to escape imprisonment. Here,
unmolested, he devoted himself for five years to social and historical research. He returned to France
in 1839 and in the following year published his
Voyage en Icarie, a book that at once took its place
by the side of Sir Thomas More's *Utopia*. Cabet
pictured in his volume an ideal society where
plenty should be a substitute for poverty and equality a remedy for class egoism. So great was the
cogency of his writing that Icaria became more
than a mere vision to hundreds of thousands in
those years of social ferment and democratic aspirations. From a hundred sources the demand arose
to translate the book into action. Cabet thereupon framed a constitution and sought the means
of founding a real Icaria. After consulting Robert
Owen, he unfortunately fell into the clutches of
some Cincinnati land speculators and chose a site
for his colony in the northeastern part of Texas.
When the announcement was made in his paper,
Le Populaire, the responses were so numerous

that Cabet believed that "more than a million coöperators" were eager for the experiment.

In February, 1848, sixty-nine young men, all carefully selected volunteers, were sent forth from Havre as the vanguard of the contemplated exodus. But the movement was halted by the turn of great events. Twenty days after the young men sailed, the French Republic was proclaimed, and in the fervor and distraction of this immediate political victory the new and distant utopia seemed to thousands less alluring than it had been before. The group of young volunteers, however, reached America. After heart-rending disillusionment in the swamps and forests of Louisiana and on the raw prairies of Texas, they made their way back to New Orleans in time to meet Cabet and four hundred Icarians, who arrived early in 1849. The Gallic instinct for factional differences soon began to assert itself in repeated division and subdivision on the part of the idealists. One-half withdrew at New Orleans to work out their individual salvation. The remainder followed Cabet to the deserted Mormon town of Nauvoo, Illinois, where vacant houses offered immediate shelter and where they enjoyed an interval of prosperity. The French genius for music, for theatricals, and for literature relieved them from the tedium that characterized most co-operative colonies. Soon their numbers increased to five hundred by accessions which, with few exceptions, were French.

But Cabet was not a practical leader. His pamphlet published in German in 1854, entitled *If I had half a million dollars*, reveals the naïveté of his mind. He wanted to find money, not to make it. The society soon became involved in a controversy in which Cabet's immediate following were outnumbered. The minority petulantly stopped working but continued to eat. "The majority decided that those who would not work should not eat . . . and gave notice that those who absented themselves from labor would be cut off from rations."[1] As a result, Cabet, in 1856, was expelled from his own Icaria! With 170 faithful adherents he went to St. Louis, and there a few days later he died. The minority buried their leader, but their faith in communal life survived this setback. At Cheltenham, a suburb of St. Louis, they acquired a small estate, where proximity to the city enabled the members to get work. Here they lived together six years before division disrupted them permanently.

[1] *Icaria, A Chapter in the History of Communism*, by Albert Shaw, p. 58.

At Nauvoo in the meantime there had been other secessions, and the property, in 1857, was in the hands of a receiver. The plucky and determined remnant, however, removed to Iowa, where on the prairie near Corning they planted a new Icaria. Here, by hard toil and in extreme poverty, but in harmony and contentment, the communists lived until, in 1876, the younger members wished to adopt advanced methods in farming, in finance, and in management. The older men, with wisdom acquired through bitter experience, refused to alter their methods. The younger party won a lawsuit to annul the communal charter. The property was divided, and again there were two Icarias, the "young party" retaining the old site and the "old party" moving on and founding New Icaria, a few miles from the old. But Old Icaria was soon split: one faction removed to California, where the Icaria-Speranza community was founded; and the other remained at Old Icaria. Both came to grief in 1888. Finally in 1895 New Icaria, then reduced to a few veterans, was dissolved by a unanimous vote of the community.

In 1854 Victor Considérant, the French socialist, planted a Fourieristic phalanx in Texas, under the

liberal patronage of J. B. A. Godin, the godfather
of Fourierism in France who founded at Guise
the only really successful phalanx. A French communistic colony was also attempted at Silkville,
Kansas. But both ventures lasted only a few
years. Since the subsidence of these French communistic experiments, there have been many sporadic attempts at founding idealistic communities
in the United States. Over fifty have been tried
since the Civil War. Nearly all were established
under American auspices and did not lure many
foreigners.

CHAPTER V

THE IRISH INVASION

AFTER the Revolution, immigrants began to filter into America from Great Britain and continental Europe. No record was kept of their arrival, and their numbers have been estimated at from 4000 to 10,000 a year, on the average. These people came nearly all from Great Britain and were driven to migrate by financial and political conditions.

In 1819 Congress passed a law requiring Collectors of Customs to keep a record of passengers arriving in their districts, together with their age, sex, occupation, and the country whence they came, and to report this information to the Secretary of State. This was the Federal Government's first effort to collect facts concerning immigration. The law was defective, yet it might have yielded valuable results had it been intelligently enforced.[1]

[1] The immigration reports were perfunctory and lacking in accuracy. Passengers were frequently listed as belonging to the

From all available collateral sources it appears that the official figures greatly understated the actual number of arrivals. Great Britain kept an official record of those who emigrated from her ports to the United States and the numbers so listed are nearly as large as the total immigration from all sources reported by the United States officials during a time when a heavy influx is known to have been coming from Germany and Switzerland.

Inaccurate as these figures are, they nevertheless are a barometer indicating the rising pressure of immigration. The first official figures show that in 1820 there arrived 8385 aliens of whom 7691 were Europeans. Of these 3614, or nearly one-half, came from Ireland. Until 1850 this proportion was maintained. Here was evidence of the first ground swell of immigration to the United States whose subsequent waves in sixty years swept to America one-half of the entire population of the Little Green Isle. Since 1820 over four and a quarter million

---

country whence they sailed. An Irishman taking passage from Liverpool was quite as likely to be reported English as Irish. Large numbers of immigrants were counted who merely landed in New York and proceeded immediately to Canada, while many thousands who landed in Canada and moved at once across the border into northern New York and the West did not appear in the reports.

Irish immigrants have found their way hither. In 1900 there were nearly five million persons in the United States descended from Irish parentage. They comprise today ten per cent of our foreign born population.

The discontent and grievances of the Irish had a vivid historical background in their own country. There were four principal causes which induced the transplanting of the race: rebellion, famine, restrictive legislation, and absentee landlordism. Every uprising of this bellicose people from the time of Cromwell onward had been followed by voluntary and involuntary exile. It is said that Cromwell's Government transported many thousand Irish to the West Indies. Many of these exiles subsequently found their way to the Carolinas, Virginia, and other colonies. After the great Irish rebellion of 1798 and again after Robert Emmet's melancholy failure in the rising of 1803 many fled across the sea. The Act of Union in 1801 brought "no submissive love for England," and constant political agitations for which the Celtic Irish need but little stimulus have kept the pathway to America populous.

The harsh penal laws of two centuries ago prescribing transportation and long terms of penal servitude were a compelling agency in driving the Irish to America. Illiberal laws against religious nonconformists, especially against the Catholics, closed the doors of political advancement in their faces, submitted them to humiliating discriminations, and drove many from the island. Finally, the selfish Navigation Laws forbade both exportation of cattle to England and the sending of foodstuffs to the colonies, dealing thereby a heavy blow to Irish agriculture. These restrictions were followed by other inhibitions until almost every industry or business in which the Irish engaged was unduly limited and controlled. It should, however, not be forgotten that these restrictions bore with equal weight upon the Ulster settlers from Scotland and England, who managed somehow to endure them successfully.

Absentee landlordism was oppressive both to the cotter's body and to his soul, for it not only bound him to perpetual poverty but kindled within him a deep sense of injustice. The historian, Justin McCarthy, says that the Irishman "regarded the right to have a bit of land, his share, exactly as other people regard the right to live." So political and economic conditions combined to feed the discontent of a people peculiarly sensitive to wrongs and swift in their resentments.

But the most potent cause of the great Irish influx into America was famine in Ireland. The economist may well ascribe Irish failure to the potato. Here was a crop so easy of culture and of such nourishing qualities that it led to over-population and all its attendant ills. The failure of this crop was indeed an "overwhelming disaster," for, according to Justin McCarthy, the Irish peasant with his wife and his family lived on the potato, and whole generations grew up, lived, married, and passed away without ever having tasted meat. When the cold and damp summer of 1845 brought the potato rot, the little, overpopulated island was facing dire want. But when the next two years brought a plant disease that destroyed the entire crop, then famine and fever claimed one quarter of the eight million inhabitants. The pitiful details of this national disaster touched American hearts. Fleets of relief ships were sent across from America, and many a shipload of Irish peasants was brought back. In 1845 over 44,821 came; 1847 saw this number rise to 105,536 and in the next year to 112,934. Rebellion following the famine swelled the number of immigrants until Ireland was left a land of old people with a fast shrinking population.

There is a prevailing notion that this influx after the great famine was the commencement of Irish migration. In reality it was only the climax. Long before this, Irishmen were found in the colonies, chiefly as indentured servants; they were in the Continental Army as valiant soldiers; they were in the western flux that filled the Mississippi Valley as useful pioneers. How many there were we do not know. As early as 1737, however, there were enough in Boston to celebrate St. Patrick's Day, and in 1762 they poured libations to their favorite saint in New York City, for the *Mercury* in announcing the meeting said, "Gentlemen that please to attend will meet with the best Usage." On March 17, 1776, the English troops evacuated Boston and General Washington issued the following order on that date:

Parole Boston

Countersign St. Patrick

The regiments under marching orders to march tomorrow morning. By His Excellency's command.

Brigadier of the Day
GEN. JOHN SULLIVAN.

Thus did the Patriot Army gracefully acknowledge the day and the people.

In 1784, on the first St. Patrick's Day after the evacuation of New York City by the British, there was a glorious celebration "spent in festivity and mirth." As the newspaper reporter put it, "the greatest unanimity and conviviality pervaded" a "numerous and jovial company."

Branches of the Society of United Irishmen were formed in American cities soon after the founding of the order in Ireland. Many veterans of '98 found their way to America, and between 1800 and 1820 many thousand followed the course of the setting sun. Their number cannot be ascertained; but there were not a few. In 1818 Irish immigrant associations were organized by the Irish in New York, Philadelphia, and Baltimore to aid the new-comers in finding work. Many filtered into the United States from Canada, Newfoundland, and the West Indies. These earlier arrivals were not composed of the abjectly poor who comprised the majority of the great exodus, and especially among the political exiles there were to be found men of some means and education.

America became extremely popular in Ireland after the Revolution of 1776, partly because the English were defeated, partly because of Irish democratic aspirations, but particularly because it

was a land of generous economic and political possibilities. The Irish at once claimed a kinship with
the new republic, and the ocean became less of a
barrier than St. George's Channel.

"The States," as they were called, became a
synonym of abundance. The most lavish reports
of plenty were sent back by the newcomers — of
meat daily, of white bread, of comfortable clothing.
"There is a great many ill conveniences here,"
writes one, "but no empty bellies." In England
and Ireland and Scotland the number of poor who
longed for this abundance exceeded the capacity
of the boats. Many who would have willingly gone
to America lacked the passage money. The Irish
peasant, born and reared in extreme poverty, was
peculiarly unable to scrape together enough to
pay his way. The assistance which he needed,
however, was forthcoming from various sources.
Friends and relatives in America sent him money;
in later years this practice was very common. Societies were organized to help those who could not
help themselves. Railroad and canal companies,
in great need of labor, imported workmen by the
thousands and advanced their passage money.
And finally, the local authorities found shipping
their paupers to another country a convenient way

of getting rid of them. England early resorted
to the same method. In 1849 the Irish poor law
guardians were given authority to borrow money
for such "assistance," as it was called. In 1881 the
Land Commission and in 1882 the Commissioner
of Public Works were authorized to advance money
for this purpose. In 1884 and 1885 over sixteen
thousand persons were thus assisted from Galway
and Mayo counties.

Long before the great Irish famine of 1846–47
America appeared like a mirage, and wondering
peasants in their dire distress exaggerated its opulence and opportunities. They braved the perils
of the sea and trusted to luck in the great new
world. The journey in itself was no small adventure. There were some sailings directly from
Ireland; but most of the Irish immigrants were
collected at Liverpool by agents not always scrup-
ulous in their dealings. A hurried inspection at
Liverpool gained them the required medical certificates, and they were packed into the ships.
Of the voyage one passenger who made the journey
from Belfast in 1795 said: "The slaves who are
carried from the coast of Africa have much more
room allowed them than the immigrants who
pass from Ireland to America, for the avarice of

captains in that trade is such that they think they can never load their vessels sufficiently, and they trouble their heads in general no more about the accommodation and storage of their passengers than of any other lumber aboard." When the great immigrant invasion of America began, there were not half enough ships for the passengers, all were cruelly overcrowded, and many were so filthy that even American port officials refused a landing before cleansing. Under such conditions sickness was a matter of course, and of the hordes who started for the promised land thousands perished on the way.[1]

Hope sustained the voyagers. But what must have been the disappointment of thousands when they landed! No ardent welcome awaited them, nor even jobs for the majority. Alas for the rosy dreams of opulence! Here was a prosaic place

---

[1] According to the *Edinburgh Review* of July, 1854, "Liverpool was crowded with emigrants, and ships could not be found to do the work. The poor creatures were packed in dense masses, in ill-ventilated and unseaworthy vessels, under charge of improper masters, and the natural results followed. Pestilence chased the fugitive to complete the work of famine. Fifteen thousand out of ninety thousand emigrants in British bottoms, in 1847, died on the passage or soon after arrival. The American vessels, owing to a stringent passenger law, were better managed, but the hospitals of New York and Boston were nevertheless crowded with patients from Irish estates."

where toil and sweat were the condition of mere existence. As the poor creatures had no means of moving on, they huddled in the ports of arrival. Almshouses were filled, beggars wandered in every street, and these peasants accustomed to the soil and the open country were congested in the cities, unhappy misfits in an entirely new economic environment. Unskilled in the handicrafts, they were forced to accept the lot of the common laborer. Fortunately, the great influx came at the time of rapid turnpike, canal, and railroad expansion. Thousands found their way westward with contractors' gangs. The free lands, however, did not lure them. They preferred to remain in the cities. New York in 1850 sheltered 133,000 Irish. Philadelphia, Boston, New Orleans, Cincinnati, Albany, Baltimore, and St. Louis, followed, in the order given, as favorite lodging places, and there was not one rapidly growing western city, such as Buffalo, Cleveland, Detroit, and Chicago, that did not have its "Irish town" or "Shanty town" where the immigrants clung together.

Their brogue and dress provoked ridicule; their poverty often threw them upon the community; the large percentage of illiteracy among them evoked little sympathy; their inclinations towards intemperance and improvidence were not neutralized by their great good nature and open-handedness; their religion reawoke historical bitterness; their genius for politics aroused jealousy; their proclivity to unite in clubs, associations, and semi-military companies made them the objects of official suspicion; and above all, their willingness to assume the offensive, to resent instantly insult or intimidation, brought them into frequent and violent contact with their new neighbors. "America for Americans" became the battle cry of reactionaries, who organized the American or "Know-Nothing" party and sought safety at the polls. While all foreign elements were grouped together, indiscriminately, in the mind of the nativist, the Irishman unfortunately was the special object of his spleen, because he was concentrated in the cities and therefore offered a visual and concrete example of the danger of foreign mass movements, because he was a Roman Catholic and thus awakened ancient religious prejudices that had long been slumbering, and because he fought back instantly, valiantly, and vehemently.

Popular suspicion against the foreigner in America began almost as soon as immigration assumed large proportions. In 1816 conservative newspapers called attention to the new problems that the Old World was thrusting upon the New: the poverty of the foreigner, his low standard of living, his illiteracy and slovenliness, his ignorance of American ways and his unwillingness to submit to them, his clannishness, the danger of his organizing and capturing the political offices and ultimately the Government. In addition to the alarmist and the prejudiced, careful and thoughtful citizens were aroused to the danger. Unfortunately, however, religious antagonisms were aroused and, as is always the case, these differences awakened the profoundest prejudices and passions of the human heart. There were many towns in New England and in the West where Roman Catholicism was unknown except as a traditional enemy of free institutions. It is difficult to realize in these days of tolerance the feelings aroused in such communities when Catholic churches, parochial schools, and convents began to appear among them; and when the devotees of this faith displayed a genius for practical politics, instinctive distrust developed into lively suspicion.

The specter of ecclesiastical authority reared itself, and the question of sharing public school moneys with parochial schools and of reading the

Bible in the public schools became a burning issue. Here and there occurred clashes that were more than barroom brawls. Organized gangs infested the cities. Both sides were sustained and encouraged by partisan papers, and on several occasions the antagonism spent themselves in riots and destruction. In 1834 the Ursuline convent at Charlestown, near Boston, was sacked and burned. Ten years later occurred the great anti-Irish riots in Philadelphia, in which two Catholic churches and a schoolhouse were burned by a mob inflamed to hysteria by one of the leaders who held up a torn American flag and shouted, "This is the flag that was trampled on by Irish papists." Prejudice accompanied fear into every city and "patented citizens" were often subject to abuse and even persecution. Tammany Hall in New York City became the political fortress of the Irish. Election riots of the first magnitude were part of the routine of elections, and the "Bloody Sixth Ward Boys" were notorious for their hooliganism on election day.

The suggestions of the nativists that paupers and criminals be excluded from immigration were not embodied into law. The movement soon was lost in the greater questions which slavery was thrusting into the foreground. When the fight

with nativism was over, the Irish were in possession of the cities.   They displayed an amazing aptitude for political plotting and organization and for
that prime essential to political success popularly
known as "mixing."   Policemen and aldermen,
ward heelers, bosses, and mayors, were known by
their brogue.   The Irish demonstrated their loyalty to the Union in the Civil War and merged
readily into American life after the lurid prejudices
against them faded.

Unfortunately, a great deal of this prejudice was
revived when the secret workings of an Irish organization in Pennsylvania were unearthed.   Among
the anthracite coal miners a society was formed,
probably about 1854, called the Molly Maguires, a
name long known in Ireland.   The members were
all Irish, professed the Roman Catholic faith, and
were active in the Ancient Order of Hibernians.
The Church, the better class of Irishmen, and the
Hibernians, however, were shocked by the doings
of the Molly Maguires and utterly disowned them.
They began their career of blackmail and bullying
by sending threats and death notices embellished
with crude drawings of coffins and pistols to those
against whom they fancied they had a grievance,
usually the mine boss or an unpopular foreman.

If the recipient did not heed the threat, he was waylaid and beaten and his family was abused. By the time of the Civil War these bullies had terrorized the entire anthracite region. Through their political influence they elected sheriffs and constables, chiefs of police and county commissioners. As they became bolder, they substituted arson and murder for threats and bullying, and they made life intolerable by their reckless brutality. It was impossible to convict them, for the hatred against an informer, inbred in every Irishman through generations of experience in Ireland, united with fear in keeping competent witnesses from the courts. Finally the president of one of the large coal companies employed James McParlan, a remarkably clever Irish detective. He joined the Mollies, somehow eluded their suspicions, and slowly worked his way into their confidence. An unusually brutal and cowardly murder in 1875 proved his opportunity. When the courts finished with the Mollies, nineteen of their members had been hanged, a large number imprisoned, and the organization was completely wiped out.

Meantime the Fenian movement served to keep the Irish in the public eye. This was no less than an attempt to free Ireland and disrupt the British

Empire, using the United States as a fulcrum, the Irish in America as the power, and Canada as the lever. James Stephens, who organized the Irish Republican Brotherhood, came to America in 1858 to start a similar movement. After the Civil War, which supplied a training school for whole regiments of Irish soldiers, a convention of Fenians was held at Philadelphia in 1865 at which an "Irish Republic" was organized, with a full complement of officers, a Congress, a President, a Secretary of the Treasury, a Secretary of War, in fact, a replica of the American Federal Government. It assumed the highly absurd and dangerous position that it actually possessed sovereignty. The luxurious mansion of a pill manufacturer in Union Square, New York, was transformed into its government house, and bonds, embellished with shamrocks and harps and a fine portrait of Wolfe Tone, were issued, payable "ninety days after the establishment of the Irish Republic." Differences soon arose, and Stephens, who had made his escape from Richmond, near Dublin, where he had been in prison, hastened to America to compose the quarrel which had now assumed true Hibernian proportions. An attempt to land an armed gang on the Island of Campo Bello on the coast of New Brunswick was frustrated; invaders from Vermont spent a night over the Canadian border before they were driven back; and for several days Fort Erie on Niagara River was held by about 1500 Fenians.[1]   General Meade was thereupon sent by the Federal authorities to put an end to these ridiculous breaches of neutrality.

Neither Meade nor any other authority, however, could stop the flow of Fenian adjectives that now issued from a hundred indignation meetings all over the land when Canada, after due trial, proceeded to sentence the guilty culprits captured in the "Battle of Limestone Ridge," as the tussle with Canadian regulars near Fort Erie was called. Newspapers abounded with tales of the most startling designs upon Canada and Britain. There then occurred a strong reaction to the Fenian movement, and the American people were led to wonder how much of truth there was in a statement made by Thomas D'Arcy McGee.[2]   "This very Fenian organization in the United States," he said, "what does it really

[1] Oberholtzer, *History of the United States since the Civil War*, vol. i, p. 526 ff.

[2] Thomas D'Arcy McGee (1825–1868), one of the leaders of the "Young Ireland" party, fled for political reasons to the United States in 1848, where he established the *New York Nation* and the *American Celt*.   When he changed his former attitude of opposition to British rule in Ireland he was attacked by the extreme

prove but that the Irish are still an alien population, camped but not settled in America, with foreign hopes and aspirations, unshared by the people among whom they live?"

The Irishman today is an integral part of every large American community. Although the restrictive legislation of two centuries ago has long been repealed and a new land system has brought great prosperity to his island home, the Irishman has not abated one whit in his temperamental attitude towards England and as a consequence some 40,000 or 50,000 of his fellow countrymen come to the United States every year. Here he has been dispossessed of his monopoly of shovel and pick by the French Canadian in New England and by the

---

Irish patriots in the United States and in consequence moved to Canada, where he founded the *New Era* and began to practice law. Subsequently, with the support of the Irish Canadians, he represented Montreal in the Parliament of United Canada (1858) and was President of the Council (1862) in the John Sandfield Macdonald Administration. When the Irish were left unrepresented in the reorganized Cabinet in the following year, McGee became an adherent of Sir John A. Macdonald, and in 1864 he was made Minister of Agriculture in the Taché-Macdonald Administration. An ardent supporter of the progressive policies of his adopted country, he was one of the Fathers of Confederation and was a member of the first Dominion Parliament in 1867. His denunciations, both in Ireland (1865) and in Canada, of the policies and activities of the Fenians led to his assassination at Ottawa on April 7, 1868.

Italian, Syrian, and Armenian in other parts of the country. He finds work in factories, for he still shuns the soil, much as he professes to love the "old sod." A great change has come over the economic condition of the second and third generation of Irish immigrants. Their remarkable buoyancy of temperament is everywhere displayed. Bridget's daughter has left the kitchen and is a school teacher, a stenographer, a saleswoman, a milliner, or a dressmaker; her son is a clerk, a bookkeeper, a traveling salesman, or a foreman. Wherever the human touch is the essential of success, there you find the Irish. That is why in some cities one-half the teachers are Irish; why salesmanship lures them; why they are the most successful walking delegates, solicitors, agents, foremen, and contractors. In the higher walks of life you find them where dash, brilliance, cleverness, and emotion are demanded. The law and the priesthood utilize their eloquence, journalism their keen insight into the human side of news, and literature their imagination and humor. They possess a positive genius for organization and management. The labor unions are led by them; and what would municipal politics be without them? The list of eminent names which they have contributed to these callings will increase as their generations multiply in the favorable American environment. But remote indeed is the day and complex must be the experience that will erase the memory of the ancient Erse proverb, which their racial temperament evoked: "Contention is better than loneliness."

CHAPTER VI

THE TEUTONIC TIDE

As the Irish wave of immigration receded the Teutonic wave rose and brought the second great influx of foreigners to American shores. A greater ethnic contrast could scarcely be imagined than that which was now afforded by these two races, the phlegmatic, plodding German and the vibrant Irish, a contrast in American life as a whole which was soon represented in miniature on the vaudeville stage by popular burlesque representations of both types. The one was the opposite of the other in temperament, in habits, in personal ambitions. The German sought the land, was content to be let alone, had no desire to command others or to mix with them, but was determined to be reliable, philosophically took things as they came, met opposition with patience, clung doggedly to a few cherished convictions, and sought passionately to possess a home and a family, to master some minute mechanical or technical detail, and to take his leisure and his amusements in his own customary way.

The reports of the Immigration Commissioner disclose the fact that well over five and a third millions of Germans migrated to America between 1823 and 1910. If to this enormous number were added those of German blood who came from Austria and the German cantons of Switzerland, from Luxemburg and the German settlements of Russia, it would reach a grand total of well over seven million Germans who have sought an ampler life in America. The Census of 1910 reports "that there were 8,282,618 white persons in the United States having Germany as their country of origin, comprising 2,501,181 who were born in Germany, 3,911,847 born in the United States both of whose parents were born in Germany, and 1,869,590 born in the United States and having one parent born in the United States and the other in Germany."[1]

[1] According to the Census of 1910 the nationality of the total number of white persons of foreign stock in the United States is distributed chiefly as follows:

Germany	8,282,618	or	25.7	per cent
Ireland	4,504,360	or	14.0	" "
Canada	2,754,615	or	8.6	" "
Russia	2,541,649	or	7.9	" "
England	2,322,442	or	7.2	" "
Italy	2,098,360	or	6.5	" "
Austria	2,001,559	or	6.2	" "

The coming of the Germans may be divided into three quite distinct migrations: the early, the middle, and the recent. The first period includes all who came before the radical ferment which began to agitate Europe after the Napoleonic wars. The Federal census of 1790 discloses 176,407 Germans living in America. But German writers usually maintain that there were from 225,000 to 250,000 Germans in the colonies at the time of the Declaration of Independence. They had been driven from the fatherland by religious persecution and economic want. Every German state contributed to their number, but the bulk of this migration came from the Palatinate, Württemberg, Baden, and Alsace, and the German cantons of Switzerland. The majority were of the peasant and artisan class who usually came over as redemptioners. Yet there were not wanting among them many persons of means and of learning.

Pennsylvania was the favorite distributing point for these German hosts. Thence they pushed

---

Furthermore, the significance of the foreign born element in the population of the United States can be gathered from the fact that, in 1910, of the 91,972,266 inhabitants of the United States, no less than 13,515,886 or 14.6 per cent were born in some other country.

southward through the beautiful Shenandoah Valley into Maryland, Virginia, and North Carolina, and northward into New Jersey. Large numbers entered at Charleston and thence went to the frontiers of South Carolina. The Mohawk Valley in New York and the Berkshires of Massachusetts harbored many. But not all of them moved inland. They were to be found scattered on the coast from Maine to Georgia. Boston, New York City, Baltimore, New Bern, Wilmington, Charleston, and Savannah, all counted Germans in their populations. However strictly these German neighborhoods may have maintained the customs of their native land, the people thoroughly identified themselves with the patriot cause and supplied soldiers, leaders, money, and enthusiasm to the cause of the Revolutionary War.

Benjamin Rush, the distinguished Philadelphia physician and publicist, one of the signers of the Declaration of Independence, wrote in 1789 a description of the Germans of Pennsylvania which would apply generally to all German settlements at that time and to many of subsequent date. The Pennsylvania German farmer, he says, was distinguished above everything else for his self-denying thrift, housing his horses and cattle in commodious, warm barns, while he and his family lived in a log hut until he was well able to afford a more comfortable house; selling his "most profitable grain, which is wheat" and "eating that which is less profitable but more nourishing, that is, rye or Indian corn"; breeding the best of livestock so that "a German horse is known in every part of the State" for his "extraordinary size or fat"; clearing his land thoroughly, not "as his English or Irish neighbors"; cultivating the most bountiful gardens and orchards; living frugally, working constantly, fearing God and debt, and rearing large families. "A German farm may be distinguished," concludes this writer, "from the farms of other citizens by the superior size of their barns, the plain but compact form of their houses, the height of their enclosures, the extent of their orchards, the fertility of their fields, the luxuriance of their meadows, and a general appearance of plenty and neatness in everything that belongs to them."[1] Rush's praise of the German mechanics is not less stinted. They were found in that day mainly as "weavers, taylors, tanners, shoe-makers, comb-makers, smiths of all kinds, butchers, paper makers, watchmakers,

[1] *An Account of the Manners of the German Inhabitants of Pennsylvania.*

and sugar bakers." Their first desire was "to become freeholders," and they almost invariably succeeded. German merchants and bankers also prospered in Philadelphia, Germantown, Lancaster, and other Pennsylvania towns. One-third of the population of Pennsylvania, Rush says, was of German origin, and for their convenience a German edition of the laws of the State was printed.

After the Revolution, a number of the Hessian hirelings who had been brought over by the British settled in America. They usually became farmers, although some of the officers taught school. They joined the German settlements, avoiding the English-speaking communities in the United States because of the resentment shown towards them. Their number is unknown. Frederick Kapp, a German writer, estimates that, of the 29,875 sent over, 12,562 never returned — but he fails to tell us how many of these remained because of Yankee bullets or bayonets.

The second period of German migration began about 1820 and lasted through the Civil War. Before 1830 the number of immigrants fluctuated between 200 and 2000 a year; in 1832 it exceeded 10,000; in 1834 it was over 17,000; three years later it reached nearly 24,000; between 1845 and 1860

9

there arrived 1,250,000, and 200,000 came during the Civil War.

There were several causes, working in close conjunction, that impelled these thousands to leave Germany. Economic disturbances doubtless turned the thoughts of the hungry and harassed to the land of plenty across the sea. But a potent cause of the great migration of the thirties and forties was the universal social and political discontent which followed in the wake of the Napoleonic wars. The German people were still divided into numberless small feudalities whose petty dukes and princes clung tenaciously to their medieval prerogatives and tyrannies. The contest against Napoleon had been waged by German patriots not only to overcome a foreign foe but to break the tyrant at home. The hope for constitutional government, for a representative system and a liberal legislation in the German States rose mightily after Waterloo. But the promises of princes made in days of stress were soon forgotten, and the Congress of Vienna had established the semblance of a German federation upon a unity of reactionary rulers, not upon a constitutional, representative basis.

The reaction against this bitter disappointment was led by the eager German youth, who, inspired by liberal ideals, now thirsted for freedom of thought, of speech, and of action. Friedrich Ludwig Jahn, a German patriot, organized everywhere *Turnvereine*, or gymnastic clubs, as a tangible form of expressing this demand. Among the students of the universities liberal patriotic clubs called *Burschenschaften* were organized, idealistic in their aims and impractical in their propaganda, where "every man with his bonnet on his head, a pot of beer in his hand, a pipe or seegar in his mouth, and a song upon his lips, never doubting but that he and his companions are training themselves to be the regenerators of Europe," vowed "the liberation of Germany." Alas for the enthusiasms of youth! In 1817 the *Burschenschaften* held a mass reunion at the Wartburg. Their boyish antics were greatly exaggerated in the conservative papers and the governments increased their vigilance. In 1819 Kotzebue, a reactionary publicist, was assassinated by a member of the Jena *Burschenschaft*, and the retaliation of the government was prompt and thoroughly Prussian — gagging of the press and of speech, dissolution of all liberal organizations, espionage, the hounding of all suspects. There seemed to remain only flight to liberal democratic America. But the suppression of the clubs did not entirely put out the

fires of constitutional desires. These smoldered
until the storms of '48 fanned them into a fitful
blaze. For a brief hour the German Democrat had
the feudal lords cowed. Frederick William, the
"romantic" Hohenzollern, promised a constitution
to the threatening mob in Berlin; the King of Saxony and the Grand Duke of Bavaria fled their capi-
tals; revolts occurred in Silesia, Posen, Hesse-Cas-
sel, and Nassau. Then struck the first great hour
of modern Prussia, as, with her heartless and disci-
plined soldiery, she restored one by one the fright-
ened dukes and princes to their prerogatives and
repressed relentlessly and with Junker rigor every
liberal concession that had crept into laws and institutions. Strangled liberalism could no longer
breathe in Germany, and thousands of her revolu-
tionists fled to America, bringing with them almost
the last vestige of German democratic leadership.

In the meantime, economic conditions in Germany remained unsatisfactory and combined with
political discontent to uproot a population and
transplant it to a new land. The desire to immi-
grate, stimulated by the transportation companies,
spread like a fever. Whole villages sold out and,
with their pastor or their physician at their head,
shipped for America. A British observer who

visited the Rhine country in 1846 commented on
"the long files of carts that meet you every mile,
carrying the whole property of these poor wretches
who are about to cross the Atlantic on the faith of
a lying prospectus." But these people were neither "poor wretches" nor dupes. They had coin
in their pockets, and in their heads a more or less
accurate knowledge of the land of their desires. At
this time the German bookshops were teeming with
little volumes giving, in the methodical Teutonic
fashion, conservative advice to prospective immigrants and rather accurate descriptions of America, with statistical information and abstracts of American laws. Many of the immigrants had further
detailed information from relatives and friends already prospering on western farms or in rapidly growing towns. This was, therefore, far from a pauper
invasion. It included every class, even broken-down
members of the nobility. The majority were, naturally, peasants and artisans, but there were multitudes of small merchants and farmers. And the political refugees included many men of substantial
property and of notable intellectual attainments.[1]

[1] J. G. Häcker, a well-informed and prosperous German who
took the journey by steerage in a sailing vessel in 1849, wrote an
instructive description of his experiences. Of his fellow passengers

Bremen was the favorite port of departure for these German emigrants to America. Havre, Hamburg, and Antwerp were popular, and even London. During the great rush every ship was overcrowded and none was over sanitary. Steerage passengers were promiscuously crowded together and furnished their own food; and the ship's crew, the captain, the agents who negotiated the voyage, and the sharks who awaited their arrival in America, all had a share in preying upon the inexperience of the immigrants. Arrived in America, these Germans were not content to settle, like dregs, in the cities on the seacoast. They were land lovers, and westward they started at once, usually in companies, sometimes as whole communities, by way of the Erie Canal and the Great Lakes, and later by the new railway lines, into Ohio, Indiana, Illinois, Michigan, Missouri, Wisconsin, and Iowa, where their instinct for the soil taught them to select the most fertile spots. Soon their log cabins and their ample barns and flourishing stock bespoke their success.

---

he said: "Our company was very mixed. There were many young people: clerks, artists, musicians, architects, miners, mechanics, men of various professions, peasants, one man seventy-eight years old, another very aged Bavarian farmer, several families of Jews, etc., and a fair collection of children."

The growing Western cities called to the skilled artisan, the small tradesman, and the intellectuals. Cincinnati early became a German center. In 1830 the Germans numbered five per cent of its population; in 1840, twenty-three per cent; and in 1869, thirty-four per cent. Milwaukee, "the German Athens," as it was once called, became the distributing point of German immigration and influence in the Northwest. Its *Gesangvereine* and *Turnvereine* became as famous as its lager beer, and German was heard more frequently than English upon its streets. St. Louis was the center of a German influence that extended throughout the Missouri Valley. Cleveland, Chicago, Detroit, Buffalo, and many of the minor towns in the Middle West received substantial additions from this migration.

Unlike the Irish, the Germans brought with them a strange language, and this proved a strong bond in that German solidarity which maintained itself in spite of the influence of their new environment. In the glow of their first enthusiasm many of the intellectuals believed they could establish a German state in America. "The foundations of a new and free Germany in the great North American Republic shall be laid by us," wrote Follenius, the dreamer, who desired to land

enough Germans in "one of the American territories to establish an essentially German state."
In 1833 the Giessener Gesellschaft, a company organized in the Grand Duchy of Hesse, grew out of
this suggestion and chose Arkansas as the site for
its colony. But unfavorable reports turned the
immigrants to Missouri, where settlements were
made. These, however, never grew into a German state but merged quite contentedly into the
prosperous American population.

A second attempt, also from Hesse, had a tragic
dénouement. A number of German nobles formed
a company called the Mainzer Adelsverein and in
1842 sent two of their colleagues to Texas to seek
out a site. The place chosen was ill-suited for a
colony, however, and the whole enterprise from beginning to end was characterized by princely in-
competence. Thousands of immigrants, lured by
the company's liberal offers and glowing prospectus, soon found themselves in dire want; many perished of disease and hunger; and the company ended in ignominious disaster. The surviving colonists in Texas, however, when they realized that
they must depend upon their own efforts, succeeded in finding work and eventually in establishing
several flourishing communities.

Finally, Wisconsin and Illinois were considered as possible sites for a Germany in America. But this ambition never assumed a concrete form. Everywhere the Americans, with their energy and organizing capacity, had preceded the incoming Germans and retained the political sovereignty of the American state.

But while they did not establish a German state, these immigrants did cling to their customs wherever they settled in considerable numbers. Especially did they retain their original social life, their *Turnvereine*, their musical clubs, their sociable beer gardens, their picnics and excursions, their churches and parochial schools. They still celebrated their Christmas and other church festivals with German cookery and *Kuchen*, and their weddings and christenings were enlivened but rarely debauched with generous libations of lager beer and wine. In the Middle West were whole regions where German was the familiar language for two generations.

There were three strata to this second German migration. The earlier courses were largely peasants and skilled artisans, those of the decade of the Civil War were mostly of the working classes, and between these came the "Forty-eighters." Upon them all, however, peasant, artisan, merchant, and intellectual, their experiences in their native land had made a deep impression. They all had a background of political philosophy the nucleus of which was individual liberty; they all had a violent distaste for the petty tyrannies and espionages which contact with their own form of government had produced; and in coming to America they all sought, besides farms and jobs, political freedom. They therefore came in humility, bore in patience the disappointments of the first rough contacts with pioneer America and its nativism, and few, if any, cherished the hope of going back to Germany. Though some of the intellectual idealists at first had indefinite enthusiasms about a *Deutschtum* in America, these visions soon vanished. They expressed no love for the governments they had left, however strong the cords of sentiment bound them to the domestic and institutional customs of their childhood.

This was to a considerable degree an idealistic migration and as such it had a lasting influence upon American life. The industry of these people and their thrift, even to paring economy, have often been extolled; but other nationalities have worked as hard and as successfully and have spent as sparingly. The special contribution to America which these Germans made lay in other qualities. Their artists and musicians and actors planted the first seeds of æsthetic appreciation in the raw West where the repertoire had previously been limited to *Money Musk*, *The Arkansas Traveler*, and *Old Dog Tray*. The liberal tendencies of German thought mellowed the austere Puritanism of the prevalent theology. The respect which these people had for intellectual attainments potently influenced the educational system of America from the kindergarten to the newly founded state universities. Their political convictions led them to espouse with ardor the cause of the Union in the war upon slavery; and their sturdy independence in partisan politics was no small factor in bringing about civil service reform. They established German newspapers by the hundreds and maintained many German schools and German colleges. They freely indulged their love for German customs. But while their sentimentalism was German, their realism was American. They considered it an honor to become American citizens. Their leaders became American leaders. Carl Schurz was not an isolated example. He was associated with a host of able, careful, constructive Germans.

The greatest quarrels of these German immigrants with American ways were over the so-called "Continental Sabbath" and the right to drink beer when and where they pleased. "Only when his beer is in danger," wrote one of the leading Forty-eighters, "does the German-American rouse himself and become a berserker." The great numbers of these men in many cities and in some of the Western States enabled them to have German taught in the public schools, though it is only fair to say that the underlying motive was liberalism rather than Prussian provincialism. Frederick Kapp, a distinguished interpreter of the spirit of these Forty-eighters, expressed their conviction when he said that those who cared to remain German should remain in Germany and that those who came to America were under solemn obligations to become Americans.

The descendants of these immigrants, the second and the third and fourth generations, are now thoroughly absorbed into every phase of American life. Their national idiosyncrasies have been modified and subdued by the gentle but relentless persistence of the English language and the robust vigor of American law and American political institutions.

After 1870 a great change came over the German immigration.   More and more industrial workers, but fewer and fewer peasants, and very rarely an intellectual or a man of substance, now appeared at Ellis Island for admission to the United States.[1] The facilities for migrating were vastly increased by the great transatlantic steamship companies. The new Germans came in hordes even outnumbering the migrations of the fifties.   From 1870 to 1910 over three and a quarter millions arrived.   The highest point of the wave, however, was reached in 1882, when 250,630 German immigrants entered the United States.   Thereafter the number rapidly subsided; the lowest ebb, in 1898, brought only 17,111, but from that time until the Great War the number of annual arrivals fluctuated between 25,000 and 40,000.

The majority of those who came in the earlier part of this period made their way to the Western lands.   The Dakotas, Nebraska, Kansas, Iowa,

[1] There were three potent reasons for this migration: financial stringency, overpopulation, and the growing rigor of the military service.   Over ten thousand processes a year were issued by the German Government in 1872 and 1873 for evasion of military duty.   Germans who had become naturalized American citizens were arrested when they returned to the Fatherland for a visit on the charge of having evaded military service.   A treaty between the two countries finally adjusted this difficulty.

and the Far West, still offered alluring opportunities. But as these lands were gradually taken, the later influx turned towards the cities. Here the immigrants not only found employment in those trades and occupations which the Germans for years had virtually monopolized, but they also became factory workers in great numbers, and many of them went into the mining regions.

It soon became apparent that the spirit of this latest migration was very different from that of the earlier ones. "I do not believe," writes a well-informed and patriotic Lutheran pastor in 1917, "that there is one among a thousand that has emigrated on account of dissatisfaction with the German Government during the last forty-five years." Humility on the part of these newcomers now gradually gave way to arrogance. Instead of appearing eager to embrace their new opportunities, they criticized everything they found in their new home. The contemptuous hauteur and provincial egotism of the modern Prussian, loathsome enough in the educated, were ridiculous in the poor immigrants. Gradually this Prussian spirit increased. In 1883 it could still be said of the three hundred German-American periodicals, daily, weekly, and monthly, that in their tone they were thoroughly American.

But ten or fifteen years later changes were apparent. In 1895 there were some five hundred German periodicals published in America, and many of the newer ones were rabidly Germanophile. The editors and owners of the older publications were dying out, and new hands were guiding the editorial pens. Often when there was no American-born German available, an editor was imported fresh from Germany. He came as a German from a new Germany — that Prussianized Germany which unmasked itself in August, 1914, and which included in its dream of power the unswerving and undivided loyalty of all Germans who had migrated. The traditional American indifference and good nature became a shield for the Machiavellian editors who now began to write not for the benefit of America but for the benefit of Germany. Political scandals, odious comparisons of American and German methods, and adroit criticisms of American ways were the daily pabulum fed to the German reader, who was left with the impression that everything in the United States was wrong, while everything in Germany was right. Before the United States entered the Great War, there was a most remarkable unanimity of expression among these German publications;

afterwards, Congress found it necessary to enact rigorous laws against them. As a result, many of them were suppressed, and many others suspended publication.

German pastors, also, were not infrequently imported and brought with them the virus of the new Prussianism. This they injected into their congregations and especially into the children who attended their catechetical instruction. German "exchange professors," in addition to their university duties, usually made a pilgrimage of the cities where the German influence was strong. The fostering of the German language became no longer merely a means of culture or an appurtenance to business but was insisted upon as a necessity to keep alive the German spirit, *der Deutsche Geist*. German parents were warned, over and over again, that once their children lost their language they would soon lose every active interest in *Kultur*. The teaching of German in the colleges and universities assumed, undisguised and unashamed, the character of Prussian propaganda. The new immigrants from Germany were carefully protected from the deteriorating effect of American contacts, and, unlike the preceding generations of German immigrants, they took very little part in politics.

Those who arrived after 1900 refused, usually, to become naturalized.

The diabolical ingenuity of the German propaganda was subsequently laid bare, and it is known today that nearly every German club, church, school, and newspaper from about 1895 onward was being secretly marshaled into a powerful Teutonic homogeneity of sentiment and public opinion. The Kaiser boasted of his political influence through the German vote. The German-American League, incorporated by Congress, had its branches in many States. Millions of dollars were spent by the Imperial German Government to corrupt the millions of German birth in America. These disclosures, when they were ultimately made, produced in the United States a sharp and profound reaction against everything Teutonic. The former indifference completely vanished and hyphen-hunting became a popular pastime. The charter of the German-American League was revoked by Congress. City after city took German from its school curriculum. Teutonic names of towns and streets were erased — half a dozen Berlins vanished overnight — and in their places appeared the names of French, British, and American heroes.

But though the names might be erased, the

German element remained. It had become incorporated into the national bone and sinew, contributing its thoroughness, stolidity, and solidity to the American stock. The power of liberal political institutions in America has been revealed, and thousands upon thousands of the sons and grandsons of German immigrants crossed the seas in 1917 and 1918 to bear aloft the starry standard upon the fields of Flanders against the arrogance and brutality of the neo-Prussians.

CHAPTER VII

THE CALL OF THE LAND

For over a century after the Revolution the great fact in American life was the unoccupied land, that vast stretch of expectant acreage lying fallow in the West. It kept the American buoyant, for it was an insurance policy against want. When his crops failed or his business grew dull, there was the West. When panic and disaster overtook him, there remained the West. When the family grew too large for the old homestead, the sons went west. And land, unlimited and virtually free, was the magnet that drew the foreign home seeker to the American shores.

The first public domain after the formation of the Union extended from the Alleghanies to the Mississippi. This area was enlarged and pushed to the Rockies by the Louisiana Purchase (1803) and was again enlarged and extended to the Pacific by the acquisition of Oregon (1846) and the Mexican cession (1848).   The total area of the United States from coast to coast then comprised 3,025,000[1] square miles, of which over two-thirds were at one time or another public domain.   Before the close of the Civil War the Government had disposed of nearly four hundred million acres but still retained in its possession an area three times as great as the whole of the territory which had been won from Great Britain in the Revolution.

The public domain was at first looked upon as a source of revenue, and a minimum price was fixed by law at $2 an acre, though this rate was subsequently (1820) lowered to $1.25 an acre.   The West always wanted liberal land laws, but the South before the Civil War, fearing that the growth of the West would give the North superior strength, opposed any such generosity.   When the North dominated Congress, the Homestead Law of 1862 provided that any person, twenty-one years of age, who was a citizen of the United States or who had declared his intention of becoming one, could obtain title to 160 acres of land by living upon it five years, making certain improvements, and paying the entry fee of ten dollars.

[1] Oberholtzer, *History of the United States since the Civil War*, vol I, p. 275.

The Government laid out its vast estate in townships six miles square, which it subdivided into sections of 640 acres and quarter sections of 160 acres. The quarter section was regarded as the public land unit and was the largest amount permitted for individual preëmption and later for a homestead. Thus was the whole world invited to go west. Under the new law, 1,160,000 acres were taken up in 1865.[1] The settler no longer had to suffer the wearisome, heart-breaking tasks that confronted the pioneer of earlier years, for the railway and steamboat had for some time taken the place of the Conestoga wagon and the fitful sailboat.

But the movement by railway and by steamboat was merely a continuation on a greater scale of what had been going on ever since the Revolution. The westward movement was begun, as we have seen, not by foreigners but by American farmers and settlers from seaboard and back country, thousands of whom, before the dawn of the nineteenth century, packed their household goods and families into covered wagons and followed the sunset trail.

The vanguard of this westward march was American, but foreign immigrants soon began to mingle

[1] Oberholtzer, *supra cit.*, p. 278.

with the caravans. At first these newcomers who heard the far call of the West were nearly all from the British Isles. Indeed so great was the exodus of these farmers that in 1816 the British journals in alarm asked Parliament to check the "ruinous drain of the most useful part of the population of the United Kingdom." Public meetings were held in Great Britain to discuss the average man's prospect in the new country. Agents of land companies found eager crowds gathered to learn particulars. Whole neighborhoods departed for America. In order to stop the exodus, the newspapers dwelt upon the hardship of the voyage and the excesses of the Americans. But, until Australia, New Zealand, and Canada began to deflect migration, the stream to the United States from England, Scotland, and Wales was constant and copious. Between 1820 and 1910 the number coming from Ireland was 4,212,169, from England 2,212,071, from Scotland 488,749, and from Wales 59,540.

What proportion of this host found their way to the farms is not known. [1] In the earlier years, the

[1] The census of 1910 discloses the fact that of the 6,361,502 farms in the United States 75 per cent were operated by native white Americans and only 10.5 per cent by foreign born whites. The foreign born were distributed as follows: Austria, 33,336; Hungary, 3827; England, 39,728; Ireland, 33,480; Scotland,

majority of the English and Scotch sought the land.
In western New York, in Ohio, Indiana, Michigan,
and contiguous States there were many Scotch and
English neighborhoods established before the Civil
War.   Since 1870, however, the incoming British
have provided large numbers of skilled mechanics
and miners, and the Welsh, also, have been drawn
largely to the coal mines.

The French Revolution drove many notables to
exile in the United States, and several attempts
were made at colonization.   The names Gallipolis
and Gallia County, Ohio, bear witness to their
French origin.   Gallipolis was settled in 1790 by
adventurers from Havre, Bordeaux, Nantes, La
Rochelle, and other French cities.   The colony was
promoted in France by Joel Barlow, an Ananias
even among land sharks, representing the Scioto
Land Company, or Companie du Scioto, one of the
numerous speculative concerns that early sought to
capitalize credulity and European ignorance of the
West.   The Company had, in fact, no title to the
lands, and the wretched colonists found themselves

10,220; Wales, 4110; France, 5832; Germany, 221,800; Holland,
13,790; Italy, 10,614; Russia, 25,788; Poland, 7228; Denmark,
28,375; Norway, 59,742; Sweden, 67,453; Switzerland, 14,333;
Canada, 61.878.

stranded in a wilderness for whose conquest they were unsuited. Of the colonists McMaster says: "Some could build coaches, some could make perukes, some could carve, others could gild with such exquisite carving that their work had been thought not unworthy of the King."[1] Congress came to the relief of these unfortunate people in 1795 and granted them twenty-four thousand acres in Ohio. The town they founded never fully realized their early dreams, but, after a bitter struggle, it survived the log cabin days and was later honored by a visit from Louis Philippe and from Lafayette. Very few descendants of the French colonists share in its present-day prosperity.

The majority of the French who came to America after 1820 were factory workers and professional people who remained in the cities. There are great numbers of French Canadians in the factory towns of New England. There are, too, French colonies in America whose inhabitants cannot be rated as foreigners, for their ancestors were veritable pioneers. Throughout the Mississippi Valley, such French settlements as Kaskaskia, Prairie du Rocher, Cahokia, and others have left much more than a geographical designation and

[1] *History of the People of the United States*, vol. VII, p. 203.

have preserved an old world aroma of quaintness and contentment.

Swiss immigrants, to the number of about 250,-000 and over 175,000 Dutch have found homes in America. The majority of the Swiss came from the German cantons of Switzerland. They have large settlements in Ohio, Wisconsin, and California, where they are very successful in dairying and stock raising. The Hollanders have taken root chiefly in western Michigan, between the Kalamazoo and Grand rivers, on the deep black bottom lands suitable for celery and market gardening. The town of Holland there, with its college and churches, is the center of Dutch influence in the United States. Six of the eleven Dutch periodicals printed in America are issued from Michigan, and the majority of newcomers (over 80,000 have arrived since 1900) have made their way to that State. These sturdy and industrious people from Holland and Switzerland readily adapt themselves to American life.

No people have answered the call of the land in recent years as eagerly as have the Scandinavians. These modern vikings have within one generation peopled a large part of the great American Northwest. In 1850 there were only eighteen thousand

Scandinavians in the United States. The tide rose rapidly in the sixties and reached its height in the eighties, until over two million Scandinavian immigrants have made America their home. They and their descendants form a very substantial part of the rural population. There are nearly half as many Norwegians in America as in Norway, which has emptied a larger proportion of its population into the American lap than any other country save Ireland. About one-fourth of the world's Swedes and over one-tenth of the world's Danes dwell in America.

The term Scandinavian is here used in the loose sense to embrace the peoples of the two peninsulas where dwell the Danes, the Norwegians, and the Swedes. These three branches of the same family have much in common, though for many years they objected to being thus rudely shaken together into one ethnic measure. The Swede is the aristocrat, the Norwegian the democrat, the Dane the conservative. The Swede, polite, vivacious, fond of music and literature, is "the Frenchman of the North," the Norwegian is a serious viking in modern dress; the Dane remains a landsman, devoted to his fields, and he is more amenable than his northern kinsmen to the cultural influence of the South.

The Norwegian, true to viking traditions, led the modern exodus. In 1825 the sloop *Restoration*, the *Mayflower* of the Norse, landed a band of fifty-three Norwegian Quakers on Manhattan. These peasants settled at first in western New York. But within a few years most of them removed to Fox River, Illinois, whither were drawn most of the Norwegians who migrated before 1850. After the Civil War, the stream rapidly rose, until nearly seven hundred thousand persons of Norwegian birth have settled in America.

The Swedish migration started in 1841, when Gustavus Unonius, a former student of the University of Upsala, founded the colony of Pine Lake, near Milwaukee. His followers have been described as a strange assortment of "noblemen, ex-army officers, merchants, and adventurers," whose experiences and talents were not of the sort that make pioneering successful. Frederika Bremer, the noted Swedish traveler, has left a description of the little cluster of log huts and the handful of people who "had taken with them the Swedish inclination for hospitality and a merry life, without sufficiently considering how long it could last." Their experiences form a romantic prelude to the great Swedish migration, which reached its height in the eighties.   Today the Swedes form the largest element in the Scandinavian influx, for well over one million have migrated to the United States.

Nearly three hundred thousand persons of Danish blood have come into the country since the Civil War.   A large number migrated from Schleswig-Holstein, after the forcible annexation of that province by Prussia in 1866, preferring the freedom of America to the tyranny of Berlin.

Whatever distinctions in language and customs may have characterized these Northern peoples, they had one ambition in common — the desire to own tillable land.   So they made of the Northwest a new Scandinavia, larger and far more prosperous than that which Gustavus Adolphus had planned in colonial days for his colony in Delaware.   One can travel today three hundred miles at a stretch across the prairies of the Dakotas or the fields of Minnesota without leaving land that is owned by Scandinavians.   They abound also in Wisconsin, Northern Illinois, Eastern Nebraska, and Kansas, and Northern Michigan.   Latterly the lands of Oregon and Washington are luring them by the thousands, while throughout the remaining West there are scattered many prosperous farms cultivated by representatives of this hardy race.   Latterly this stream of Scandinavians has thinned to about one-half its former size.   In 1910, 48,000 came; in 1911, 42,000; in 1912, 27,000; in 1913, 33,000.   The later immigrant is absorbed by the cities, or sails upon the Great Lakes or in the coastwise trade, or works in lumber camps or mines.   Wherever you find a Scandinavian, however, he is working close to nature, even though he is responding to the call of the new industry.

It is the consensus of opinion among competent observers that these northern peoples have been the most useful of the recent great additions to the American race.   They were particularly fitted by nature for the conquest of the great area which they have brought under subjugation, not merely because of their indomitable industry, perseverance, honesty, and aptitude for agriculture, but because they share with the Englishman and the Scotchman the instinct for self-government.   Above all, the Scandinavian has never looked upon himself as an exile.   From the first he has considered himself an American.   In Minnesota and Dakota, the Norse pioneer often preceded local government. "Whenever a township became populous enough to have a name as well as a number on the surveyor's map, that question was likely to be determined by the people on the ground, and such names as Christiana, Swede Plain, Numedal, Throndhjem, and Vasa leave no doubt that Scandinavians officiated at the christening." These people proceeded with the organizing of the local government and, "except for the peculiar names, no one would suspect that the town-makers were born elsewhere than in Massachusetts or New York."[1] This, too, in spite of the fact that they continued the use of their mother tongue, for not infrequently election notices and even civic ordinances and orders were issued in Norwegian or Swedish. In 1893 there were 146 Scandinavian newspapers, and their number has since greatly increased.

In politics the Norseman learned his lesson quickly. Governors, senators, and representatives in Congress give evidence to a racial clannishness that has more than once proven stronger than party allegiance. Yet with all their influence in the Northwest, they have not insisted on unreasonable race recognition, as have the Germans in Wisconsin and other localities. Minnesota and Dakota have established classes in "the Scandinavian language" in their state universities,

[1] K. C. Babcock, *The Scandinavian Element in the United States,* p. 143.

evidently leaving it to be decided as an academic question which is *the* Scandinavian language. Without brilliance, producing few leaders,
the Norseman represents the rugged common-
place of American life, avoiding the catastrophes
of a soaring ambition on the one hand and the pit-
falls of a jaded temperamentalism on the other.
Bent on self-improvement, he scrupulously patro-
nizes farmers' institutes, high schools, and exten-
sion courses, and listens with intelligent patience
to lectures that would put an American audience
to sleep. This son of the North has greatly but-
tressed every worthy American institution with
the stern traditional virtues of the tiller of the soil.
Strength he gives, if not grace, and that at a time
when all social institutions are being shaken to
their foundations.

Among the early homesteaders in the upper Mississippi Valley there were a substantial number of
Bohemians. In Nebraska they comprise nine per
cent of the foreign born population, in Oklahoma
seven per cent, and in Texas over six per cent.
They began migrating in the turbulent forties.
They were nearly all of the peasant class, neat, industrious and intelligent, and they usually settled
in colonies where they retained their native tongue

and customs. They were opposed to slavery and many enlisted in the Union cause.

Among the Polish immigrants who came to America before 1870, many settled on farms in Illinois, Wisconsin, Texas, and other States. They proved much more clannish than the Bohemians and more reluctant to conform to American customs.

Many farms in the Northwest are occupied by Finns, of whom there were in 1910 over two hundred thousand in the United States. They are a Tatar race, with a copious sprinkling of Swedish blood. Illiteracy is rare among them. They are eager patrons of night schools and libraries and have a flourishing college near Duluth. They are eager for citizenship and are independent in politics. The glittering generalities of Marxian socialism seem peculiarly alluring to them; and not a few have joined the I. W. W. Drink has been their curse, but a strong temperance movement has recently made rapid headway among them. They are natural woodmen and wield the axe with the skill of our own frontiersmen. Their peculiar houses, made of neatly squared logs, are features of every Finnish settlement. All of the North European races and a few from Southern and Eastern Europe have contributed to the American rural population; yet the Census of 1910 disclosed the fact that of the 6,361,502 white farm operators in the United States, 75 per cent were native American and only 10.5 per cent were foreign born.

CHAPTER VIII

THE CITY BUILDERS

"WHAT will happen to immigration when the public domain has vanished?" was a question frequently asked by thoughtful American citizens. The question has been answered: the immigrant has become a job seeker in the city instead of a home seeker in the open country. The last three decades have witnessed "the portentous growth of the cities" — and they are cities of a new type, cities of gigantic factories, towering skyscrapers, electric trolleys, telephones, automobiles, and motor trucks, and of fetid tenements swarming with immigrants. The immigrants, too, are of a new type. When Henry James revisited Boston after a long absence, he was shocked at the "gross little foreigners" who infested its streets, and he said it seemed as if the fine old city had been wiped with "a sponge saturated with the foreign mixture and passed over almost everything I remembered and might have still recovered."[1]

Until 1882 the bulk of immigration, as we have seen, came from the north of Europe, and these immigrants were kinsmen to the American and for the most part sought the country. The new immigration, however, which chiefly sought the cities, hailed from southern and eastern Europe. It has shown itself alien in language, custom, in ethnic affinities and political concepts, in personal standards and assimilative ambitions. These immigrants arrived usually in masculine hordes, leaving women and children behind, clinging to their own kind with an apprehensive mistrust of all things American, and filled with the desire to extract from this fabulous mine as much gold as possible and then to return to their native villages. Yet a very large number of those who have gone home to Europe have returned to America with bride or family. As a result the larger cities of the United States are congeries of foreign quarters, whose alarming fecundity fills the streets with progeny and whose polyglot chatter on pay night turns even many a demure New England town into a veritable babel.

[1] This lament of Henry James's is cited by E. A. Ross in *The Old World in the New*, p. 101.

There are in the United States today roughly eight or ten millions of these new immigrants. A line drawn southward from Minneapolis to St. Louis and thence eastward to Washington would embrace over four-fifths of them, for most of the great American cities lie in this northeastern corner of the land. Whence come these millions? From the vast and mysterious lands of the Slavs, from Italy, from Greece, and from the Levant.

The term Slav covers a welter of nationalities whose common ethnic heritage has long been concealed under religious, geographical, and political diversities and feuds. They may be divided into North Slavs, including Bohemians, Poles, Ruthenians, Slovaks, and "Russians," and South Slavs, including Bulgarians, Serbians and Montenegrins, Croatians, Slovenians, and Dalmatians. As one writer on these races says, "It is often impossible in America to distinguish these national groups. . . . Yet the differences are there. . . . In American communities they have their different churches, societies, newspapers, and a separate social life. . . . The Pole wastes no love on the Russian, nor the Ruthenian on the Pole, and a person who acts in ignorance of these facts, a missionary for instance, or a political boss, or a trade union organizer, may find himself in the position of a host who should innocently invite a Fenian from Cork County to hobnob with an Ulster Orangeman on the ground that both were Irish."[1]

The Bohemians (including the Moravians) are the most venturesome and the most enlightened of the great Slav family. Many of them came to America in the seventeenth century as religious pilgrims; more came as political refugees after 1848; and since 1870, they have come in larger numbers, seeking better economic conditions. All told, they numbered over 220,000, from which it may be estimated that there are probably today half a million persons of Bohemian parentage in the United States. Chicago alone shelters over 100,000 of these people, and Cleveland 45,000. These immigrants as a rule own the neat, box-like houses in which they live, where flower-pots and tiny gardens bespeak a love of growing things, and lace curtains, carpets, and center tables testify to the influence of an American environment. The Bohemians are much given to clubs, lodges, and societies, which usually have rooms over Bohemian saloons. The second generation is prone to free thinking and has a weakness for radical socialism.

[1] Emily Greene Balch, *Our Slavic Fellow Citizens*, p. 8–9.

The Bohemians are assiduous readers, and illiteracy is almost unknown among them. They support many periodicals and several thriving publishing houses. They cling to their language with a religious fervor. Their literature and the history which it preserves is their pride. Yet this love of their own traditions is no barrier, apparently, to forming strong attachments to American institutions. The Bohemians are active in politics, and in the cities where they congregate they see that they have their share of the public offices. There are more highly skilled workmen among them than are to be found in any other Slavic group; and the second generation of Bohemians in America has produced many brilliant professional men and successful business men. As one writer puts it: "The miracle which America works upon the Bohemians is more remarkable than any other of our national achievements. The downcast look so characteristic of them in Prague is nearly gone, the surliness and unfriendliness disappear, and the young Bohemian of the second or third generation is as frank and open as his neighbor with his Anglo-Saxon heritage."[1]

The bitter political and racial suppression that

[1] Edward A. Steiner, *On the Trail of the Immigrant*, p. 228.

made the Bohemian surly and defiant seem, on the other hand, to have left the Polish peasant stolid, patient, and very illiterate. Polish settlements were made in Texas and Wisconsin in the fifties and before 1880 a large number of Poles were scattered through New York, Pennsylvania, and Illinois. Since then great numbers have come over in the new migrations until today, it is estimated, at least three million persons of Polish parentage live in the United States.[1] The men in the earlier migrations frequently settled on the land; the recent comers hasten to the mines and the metal working centers, where their strong though untrained hands are in constant demand.

The majority of the Poles have come to America to stay. They remain, however, very clannish and according to the Federal Industrial Commission, without the "desire to fuse socially." The recent Polish immigrant is very circumscribed in his mental horizon, clings tenaciously to his language, which he hears exclusively in his home and his

[1] This is an estimate made by the Reverend W. X. Kruszka of Ripon, Wisconsin, as reported by E. G. Balch in *Our Slavic Fellow Citizens*, p. 262. Of this large number, Chicago claims 350,000; New York City, 250,000; Buffalo, 80,000; Milwaukee, 75,000; Detroit, 75,000; while at least a dozen other cities have substantial Polish settlements. These numbers include the suburbs of each city.

church, his lodge, and his saloon, and is unresponsive to his American environment. Not until the second and third generation is reached does the spirit of American democracy make headway against his lethal stolidity. Now that Poland has been made free as a result of the Great War, it may be that the Pole's inherited indifference will give way to national aspirations and that, in the resurrection of his historic hope of freedom, he will find an animating stimulant.

The Pole, however, is more independent and progressive than the Slovak, his brother from the northeastern corner of Hungary. For many generations this segment of the Slav race has been pitifully crushed. Turks, Magyars, and Huns have taken delight in oppressing him. An early, sporadic migration of Slovaks to America received a sudden impulse in 1882. About 200,000 have come since then, and perhaps twice that number of persons of Slovak blood now dwell in the mining and industrial centers of the United States. Many of them, however, return to their native villages. They keep aloof from things American and only too often prefer to live in squalor and ignorance. Their social life is centered in the church, the saloon, and the lodge. It is asserted that their numerous organizations have a membership of over 100,000, and that there were almost as many Slovak newspapers in America as in Hungary.[1]

Little Russia, the seat of turmoil, is the home of the Ruthenians, or Ukranians. They are also found in southeastern Galicia, northern Hungary, and in the province of Bukowina. They have migrated from all these provinces and about 350,000, it is estimated, now reside in the United States. They, too, are birds of passage, working in the mines and steel mills for the coveted wages that shall free them from debt at home and insure their independence. Such respite as they take from their labors is spent in the saloon, in the club rooms over the saloon, or in church, where they hear no English speech and learn nothing of American ways.

It is impossible to estimate the total number of Russian Slavs in the United States, as the census figures until recently included as "Russian" all nationalities that came from Russia. They form the smallest of the Slavic groups that have migrated to America. From 1898 to 1909 only 66,282 arrived, about half of whom settled in Pennsylvania and New York. It is surprising to note,

[1] This is accounted for by the fact that the Hungarian Government rigorously censored Slovak publications.

however, that every State in the Union except
Utah and every island possession except the Philippines has received a few of these immigrants. The
Director of Emigration at St. Petersburg in 1907
characterized these people as "hardy and industrious," and "though illiterate they are intelligent
and unbigoted."[1]

So much in brief for the North Slavs. Of the
South Slavs, the Bulgarians possess racial characteristics which point to an intermixture in the remote past with some Asiatic strain, perhaps a
Magyar blend. Very few Bulgarian immigrants,
who come largely from Macedonia, arrived before
the revolution of 1904, when many villages in
Monastir were destroyed. For some years they
made Granite City, near St. Louis, the center of
their activities but, like the Serbians, they are now
well scattered throughout the country. In Seattle,
Butte, Chicago, and Indianapolis they form considerable colonies. Many of them return yearly
to their native hills, and it is too early to determine how fully they desire to adapt themselves to
American ways.

---

[1] Since the Russo-Japanese War, Siberia has absorbed great
numbers of Russian immigrants. This accounts for the small
number that have come to America.

Montenegro, Serbia, and Bulgaria, countries that have been thrust forcibly into the world's vision by the Great War, have sent several hundred thousand of their hardy peasantry to the United States. The Montenegrins and Serbians, who comprise three-fourths of this migration, are virtually one in speech and descent. They are to be found in New England towns and in nearly every State from New York to Alaska, where they work in the mills and mines and in construction gangs. The response which these people make to educational opportunities shows their high cultural possibilities.

The Croatians and Dalmatians, who constitute the larger part of the southern Slav immigration, are a sturdy, vigorous people, and splendid specimens of physical manhood. The Dalmatians are a seafaring folk from the Adriatic coast, whose sailors may be found in every port of the world. The Dalmatians have possessed themselves of the oyster fisheries near New Orleans and are to be found in Mississippi making staves and in California making wine. In many cities they manage restaurants. The exceptional shrewdness of the Dalmatians is in bold contrast to their illiteracy. They get on amazingly in spite of their lack of education. Once they have determined to remain in this country, they take to American ways more readily than do the other southern Slavs.

Croatia, too, has its men of the sea, but in America most of the immigrants of this race are to be found in the mines and coke furnaces of Pennsylvania and West Virginia. In New York City there are some 15,000 Croatian mechanics and longshoremen. The silver and copper mines of Montana also employ a large number of these people. It is estimated that fully one-half of the Croatians return to their native hills and that they contribute yearly many millions to the home-folks.

From the little province of Carniola come the Slovenians, usually known as "Griners" (from the German *Krainer*, the people of the Krain), a fragment of the Slavic race that has become much more assimilated with the Germans who govern them than any other of their kind. Their national costume has all but vanished and with it the virile traditions of their forefathers. They began coming to America in the sixties, and in the seventies they founded an important colony at Joliet, Illinois. Since 1892 their numbers have increased rapidly, until today about 100,000 live in the United States. Over one-half of these immigrants are to be found

In the steel and mining towns of Pennsylvania, Ohio, and Illinois, where the large majority of them are unskilled workmen. Among the second generation, however, are to be found a number of successful merchants.

All these numerous peoples have inherited in common the impassive, patient temperament and the unhappy political fate of the Slav. Their countries are mere eddies left by the mighty currents of European conquest and reconquest, backward lands untouched by machine industry and avoided by capital, whose only living links with the moving world are the birds of passage, the immigrants who flit between the mines and cities of America and these isolated European villages. Held together by national costume, song, dance, festival, traditions, and language, these people live in the pale glory of a heroic past. Most of those who come to America are peasants who have been crushed by land feudalism, kept in ignorance by political intolerance, and bound in superstition by a reactionary ecclesiasticism. The brutality with which they treat their women, their disregard for sanitary measures, and their love for strong drink are evidences of the survival of medievalism in the midst of modern life, as are their notions of class prerogative and their concept of the State. Buffeted by the world, their language suppressed, their nationalism reviled, poor, ignorant, unskilled, these children of the open country come to the ugliest spots of America, the slums of the cities, and the choking atmosphere of the mines. Here, crowded in their colonies, jealously shepherded by their church, neglected by the community, they remain for an entire generation immune to American influences. According to estimates given by Emily G. Balch,[1] between four and six million persons of Slavic descent are now dwelling among us, and their fecundity is amazing. Equally amazing is the indifference of the Government and of Americans generally to the menace involved in the increasing numbers of these inveterate aliens to institutions that are fundamentally American.

The Lithuanians and Magyars are often classed with the Slavs. They hotly resent this inclusion, however, for they are distinct racial strains of ancient lineage. An adverse fate has left the Lithuanian little of his old civilization except his language. Political and economic suppression has made sad havoc of what was once a proud and

[1] *Our Slavic Fellow Citizens*, p. 280.

prosperous people.   Most of them are now crowded into the Baltic province that bears their name, and they are reduced to the mental and economic level of the Russian moujik.   In 1868 a famine drove the first of these immigrants to America, where they were soon absorbed by the anthracite mines of Pennsylvania.   They were joined in the seventies by numbers of army deserters.   The hard times of the nineties caused a rush of young men to the western El Dorado.   Since then the influx has steadily continued until now over 200,000 are in America. They persistently avoid agriculture and seek the coal mine and the factory.   The one craft in which they excel is tailoring, and they proudly boast of being the best dressed among all the Eastern-European immigrants.   The one mercantile ambition which they have nourished is to keep a saloon. Drinking is their national vice; and they measure the social success of every wedding, christening, picnic, and jollification by its salvage of empty beer kegs.

Over 338,000 Magyars immigrated to the United States during the decade ending 1910.   These brilliant and masterful folk are a Mongoloid blend that swept from the steppes of Asia across eastern Europe a thousand years ago.   As the wave receded, the Magyars remained dominant in beautiful and fertile Hungary, where their aggressive nationalism still brings them into constant rivalry on the one hand with the Germans of Austria and on the other with the Slavs of Hungary. The immigrants to America are largely recruited from the peasantry. They almost invariably seek the cities, where the Magyar neighborhoods can be easily distinguished by their scrupulously neat housekeeping, the flower beds, the little patches of well-swept grass, the clean children, and the robust and tidy women. Among them is less illiteracy than in any other group from eastern and southern Europe, excepting the Finns, who are their ethnic brothers. As a rule they own their own homes. They learn the English language quickly but unfortunately acquire with it many American vices. Drinking and carousing are responsible for their many crimes of personal violence. They are otherwise a sociable, happy people, and the cafés kept by Hungarians are islands of social jollity in the desert of urban strife.

In bold contrast to these ardent devotees of nationalism, the Jew, the man of no country and of all countries, is an American immigrant still to be considered. By force of circumstance he became a city dweller; he came from the European city; he remained in the American city; and all attempts to colonize Jews on the land have failed. The doors of this country have always been open to him. At the time of the Revolution several thousand Jews dwelt in American towns. By 1850 the number had increased to 50,000 and by the time of the Civil War to 150,000. The persecutions of Czar Alexander III in the eighties swelled the number to over 400,000, and the political reactions of the nineties added over one million. Today at least one fifth of the ten million Jews in the world live in American cities.

The first to seek a new Zion in this land were the Spanish-Portuguese Jews, who came as early as 1655. They remain a select aristocracy among their race, clinging to certain ritualistic characteristics and retaining much of the pride which their long contact with the Spaniard has engendered. They are found almost exclusively in the eastern cities, as successful bankers, merchants, and professional men. There next came on the wave of the great German immigration the German Jews. They are to be found in every city, large and small, engaged in mercantile pursuits, especially in the drygoods and the clothing business. Nearly all of the prominent Jews in America have come from this stock — the great bankers, financiers, lawyers, merchants, rabbis, scholars, and public men. It was, indeed, from their broad-minded scholars that there originated the widespread liberal Judaism which has become a potent ethical force in our great cities.

The Austrian and Hungarian Jews followed. The Jews had always received liberal treatment in Hungary, and their mingling with the social Magyars had produced the type of the coffee-house Jew, who loved to reproduce in American cities the conviviality of Vienna and Budapest but who did not take as readily to American ways as the German Jew. Most of the Jews from Hungary remained in New York, although Chicago and St. Louis received a few of them. In commercial life they are traders, pawnbrokers, and peddlers, and control the artificial-flower and passementerie trade.

By far the largest group are the latest comers, the Russian Jews. "Ultra orthodox," says Edward A. Steiner, "yet ultra radical; chained to the past, and yet utterly severed from it; with religion permeating every act of life, or going to the other extreme and having 'none of it'; traders by instinct, and yet among the hardest manual laborers of our great cities. A complex mass in which great things are yearning to express themselves, a brooding mass which does not know itself and does not lightly disclose itself to the outside."[1] Nearly a million of these people are crowded into the New York ghettos. Large numbers of them engage in the garment industries and the manufacture of tobacco. They graduate also into junk-dealers, pawnbrokers, and peddlers, and are soon on their way "up town." Among them socialism thrives, and the second generation displays an unseemly haste to break with the faith of its fathers.

The Jews are the intellectuals of the new immigration. They invest their political ideas with vague generalizations of human amelioration. They cannot forget that Karl Marx was a Jew: and one wonders how many Trotzkys and Lenines are being bred in the stagnant air of their reeking ghettos. It remains to be seen whether they will be willing to devote their undoubted mental capacities to other than revolutionary vagaries or to gainful pursuits, for they have a tendency to commercialize everything they touch. They have

[1] *On the Trail of the Immigrant*, p. 27.

shown no reluctance to enter politics; they learn English with amazing rapidity, throng the public schools and colleges, and push with characteristic zeal and persistence into every open door of this liberal land.

From Italy there have come to America well over three million immigrants. For two decades before 1870 they filtered in at the average rate of about one thousand a year; then the current increased to several thousand a year; and after 1880 it rose to a flood.[1] Over two-thirds of these Italians live in the larger cities; one-fourth of them are crowded into New York tenements.[2] Following in order, Philadelphia, Chicago, Boston, New Orleans, Cleveland, St. Louis, Baltimore, Detroit, Portland, and Omaha have their Italian quarters, all characterized by overcrowded boarding houses and tenements, vast hordes of children, here and there an Italian bakery and grocery, on every corner a saloon, and usually a private bank with a

[1] The census figures show that approximately half the Italian immigrants return to their native land. American officers in the Great War were surprised to find so many Italian soldiers who spoke English. In 1910 there remained in the United States only 1,343,000 Italians who were born in Italy, and the total number of persons of Italian stock in the United States was 2,098,000.

[2] According to the Census of 1910 there were 544,000 Italians in New York City

steamship agency and the office of the local *padrone*. Scores of the lesser cities also have their Italian contingent, usually in the poorest and most neglected part of the town, where gaudily painted door jambs and window frames and wonderfully prosperous gardens proclaim the immigrant from sunny Italy. Not infrequently an old warehouse, store, or church is transformed into an ungainly and evil-odored barracks, housing scores of men who do their own washing and cooking. Those who do not dwell in the cities are at work in construction camps — for the Italian has succeeded the Irishman as the knight of the pick and shovel. The great bulk of these swarthy, singing, hopeful young fellows are peasants, unskilled of hand but willing of heart. Nearly every other one is unable to read or write. They have not come for political or religious reasons but purely as seekers for wages, driven from the peasant villages by overpopulation and the hazards of a precarious agriculture.

They have come in two distinct streams: one from northern Italy, embracing about one-fifth of the whole; the other from southern Italy. The two streams are quite distinct in quality. Northern Italy is the home of the old masters in art and literature and of a new industrialism that is bringing renewed prosperity to Milan and Turin. Here the virile native stock has been strengthened with the blood of its northern neighbors. They are a capable, creative, conservative, reliable race. On the other hand, the hot temper of the South has been fed by an infusion of Greek and Saracen blood. In Sicily this strain shows at its worst. There the vendetta flourishes; and the Camorra and its sinister analogue, the Black Hand, but too realistically remind us that thousands of these swarthy criminals have found refuge in the dark alleys of our cities. Even in America the Sicilian carries a dirk, and the "death sign" in a court room has silenced many a witness. The north Italians readily identify themselves with American life. Among them are found bakers, barbers, and marble cutters, as well as wholesale fruit and olive oil merchants, artists, and musicians. But the south Italian is a restless, roving creature, who dislikes the confinement and restraint of the mill and factory. He is found out of doors, making roads and excavations, railways, skyscrapers, and houses. If he has a liking for trade he trundles a pushcart filled with fruit or chocolates; or he may turn a jolly hurdy-gurdy or grind scissors. In spite of his native sociability, the south Italian is very slow to take to American ways. As a rule, he comes here intending to go back when he has made enough money. He has the air of a sojourner. He is picturesque, volatile, and incapable of effective team work.

About 300,000 Greeks have come to America between 1908 and 1917, nearly all of them young men, escaping from a country where they had meat three times a year to a land where they may have it three times a day. "The whole Greek world," says Henry P. Fairchild, writing in 1911, "may be said to be in a fever of emigration. . . . The strong young men with one accord are severing home ties, leaving behind wives and sweethearts, and thronging to the shores of America in search of opportunity and fortune." Every year they send back handsome sums to the expectant family. Business is an instinct with the Greek, and he has almost monopolized the ice cream, confectionery, and retail fruit business, the small florist shops and bootblack stands in scores of towns, and in every large city he is running successful restaurants. As a factory operative he is found in the cotton mills of New England, but he prefers merchandizing to any other calling.

Years ago when New Bedford was still a whaling port a group of Portuguese sailors from the Azores settled there. This formed the nucleus of the Portuguese immigration which, in the last decade, included over 80,000 persons. Two-thirds of these live in New England factory towns, the remaining third, strange to say, have found their way to the other side of the continent, where they work in the gardens and fruit orchards of California. New Bedford is still the center of their activity. They are a hard-working people whose standard of living, according to official investigations "is much lower than that of any other race," of whom scarcely one in twenty become citizens, and who evince no interest in learning or in manual skill.

Finally, American cities are extending the radius of their magnetism and are drawing ambitious tradesmen and workers from the Levant. Over 100,000 have come from Arabia, Syria, Armenia, and Turkey. The Armenians and Syrians, forming the bulk of this influx, came as refugees from the brutalities of the Mohammedan régime. The Levantine is first and always a bargainer. His little bazaars and oriental rug shops are bits of Cairo and Constantinople, where you are privileged to haggle over every purchase in true oriental style. Even the peddlers of lace and drawn-work find it hard to accustom themselves to the occidental idea of a market price. With all their cunning as traders, they respect learning, prize manual skill, possess a fine artistic sense, and are law-abiding. The Armenians especially are eager to become American citizens. Since the settlement of the Northwestern lands, many thousands of Scandinavians and Finns have flocked to the cities, where they are usually employed as skilled craftsmen.[1]

Thus the United States, in a quarter of a century, has assumed a cosmopolitanism in which the early German and Irish immigrants appear as veteran

[1] The Census of 1910 gives the following distribution of the American white population by percentages:

Location	Native stock	Native born of Foreign or mixed parentage	Foreign born
Rural districts	64.1	13.3	7.5
Cities 2,500 – 10,000	57.5	20.6	13.9
" 10,000– 25,000	50.4	24.6	17.4
" 25,000–100,000	45.9	26.5	20.2
" 100,000–500,000	38.9	31.3	22.1
" 500,000 and over	25.6	37.2	33.6

The native white element predominates in the country but is only a fraction of the population in the larger cities.

Americans. This is not a stationary cosmopolitanism, like that of Constantinople, the only great city in Europe that compares with New York, Chicago, or Boston in ethnic complexity. It is a shifting mass. No two generations occupy the same quarters. Even the old rich move "up town" leaving their fine houses, derelicts of a former splendor, to be divided into tenements where six or eight Italian or Polish families find ample room for themselves and a crowd of boarders.

Thousands of these migratory beings throng the steerage of transatlantic ships every winter to return to their European homes. The steamship companies, whose enterprise is largely responsible for this flow of populations, reap their harvest; and many a decaying village buried in the southern hills of Europe, or swept by the winds of the great Slav plains, owes its regeneration ultimately to American dollars.

They pay the price of their success, these flitting beings, links between distant lands and our own. The great maw of mine and factory devours thousands. Their lyric tribal songs are soon drowned by the raucous voices of the city; their ancient folk-dances, meant for a village green, not for a reeking dance-hall, lose here their native grace;

and the quaint and picturesque costumes of the European peasant give place to American store clothes, the ugly badge of equality.

The outward bound throng holds its head high, talks back at the steward, and swaggers. It has become "American." The restless fever of the great democracy is in its veins. Most of those who return home will find their way back with others of their kind to the teeming hives and the coveted fleshpots they are leaving. And again they will tax the ingenuity of labor unions, political and social organizations, schools, libraries, and churches, in the endeavor to transform medieval peasants into democratic peers.

CHAPTER IX

THE ORIENTAL

AMERICA, midway between Europe and Asia, was destined to be the meeting-ground of Occident and Orient. It was in the exciting days of '49 that gold became the lodestone to draw to California men from the oriental lands across the Pacific. The Chinese for the moment overcame their religious aversion to leaving their native haunts and, lured by the promise of fabulous wages, made their way to the "gold hills." Of the three hundred thousand who came to America during the three decades of free entry, the large majority were peasants from the rural districts in the vicinity of Canton. They were thrifty, independent, sturdy, honest young men who sought the great adventure unaccompanied by wife or family. Chinese tradition forbade the respectable woman to leave her home, even with her husband; and China was so isolated from the world, so encrusted in her own traditions that out of her uncounted millions even the paltry thousands of peasants and workmen who filtered through the port of Canton into the great world were bound by ancient precedent as firmly as if they had remained at home. They invariably planned to return to the Celestial Empire and it was their supreme wish that, if they died abroad, their bodies be buried in the land of their ancestors.

The Chinaman thus came to America as a workman adventurer, not as a prospective citizen. He preserved his queue, his pajamas, his chopsticks, and his joss in the crude and often brutal surroundings of the mining camp. He maintained that gentle, yielding, unassertive character which succumbs quietly to pressure at one point, only to reappear silently and unobtrusively in another place. In the wild rough and tumble of the camp, where the outlaw and the bully found congenial refuge, the celestial did not belie his name. He was indeed of another world, and his capacity for patience, his native dignity without suspicion of hauteur, baffled the loud self-assertion of the Irish and the Anglo-Saxon.

During the first years of the gold rush, the Chinaman was welcome in California because he was necessary. He could do so many things that the miner disdained or found no time to do. He could cook and wash, and he could serve. He was a rare gardener and a patient day laborer. He could learn a new trade quickly. In the city he became a useful domestic servant at a time when there were very few women. In all his tasks he was neat and had a genius for noiselessly minding his own business.

As the number of miners increased, race prejudice asserted itself. "California for Americans" came to be a slogan that reflected their feelings against Mexicans, Spanish-Americans, and Chinese in the mines. Race riots, often instigated by men who had themselves but recently immigrated to America, were not infrequent. In these disorders the Chinese were no match for the aggressors and in consequence were forced out of many good mining claims.

The labor of the cheap and faithful Chinese appealed to the business instincts of the railroad contractors who were constructing the Pacific railways and they imported large numbers. In 1866 a line of steamships was established to run regularly between Hong Kong and San Francisco. In 1869 the first transcontinental railway was completed and American laborers from the East began to flock to

California, where they immediately found themselves in competition with the Mongolian standard of living. Race rivalry soon flared up and the anti-Chinese sentiment increased as the railroads neared completion and threw more and more of the oriental laborers into the general labor market. Chinese were hustled out of towns. Here and there violence was done. For example, in the Los Angeles riots of October 24, 1871, fifteen Chinamen were hanged and six were shot by the mob.

This prejudice, based primarily upon the Chinaman's willingness to work long hours for little pay and to live in quarters and upon fare which an Anglo-Saxon would find impossible, was greatly increased by his strange garb, language, and customs. The Chinaman remained in every essential a foreigner. In his various societies he maintained to some degree the patriarchal government of his native village. He shunned American courts, avoided the Christian religion, rarely learned much of the English language, and displayed no desire to become naturalized. Instead of sympathy in the country of his sojourn he met discrimination, jealousy, and suspicion. For many years his testimony was not permitted in the courts. His contact with only the rough frontier life failed to reveal to him the gentle amenities of the white man's faith, and everywhere the upper hand seemed turned against him. So he kept to himself, and this isolation fed the rumors that were constantly poisoning public opinion. Chinatown in the public mind became a synonym for a nightmare of filth, gambling, opium-smoking, and prostitution.

Alarm was spreading among Americans concerning the organizations of the Chinese in the United States. Of these, the Six Companies were the most famous. Mary Roberts Coolidge, after long and careful research, characterized these societies as "the substitute for village and patriarchal association, and although purely voluntary and benevolent in their purpose, they became, because of American ignorance and prejudice, the supposed instruments of tyranny over their countrymen."[1] They each had a club house, where members were registered and where lodgings and other accommodations were provided. The largest in 1877 had a membership of seventy-five thousand; the smallest, forty-three thousand. The Chinese also maintained trade guilds similar in purpose to the American trade union. Private or secret societies also flourished among them, some for good purposes,

[1] *Chinese Immigration*, p. 402

others for illicit purposes. Of the latter the High-binders or Hatchet Men became the most notorious, for they facilitated the importation of Chinese prostitutes. Many of these secret societies thrived on blackmail, and the popular antagonism to the Six Companies was due to the outrages committed by these criminal associations.

When the American labor unions accumulated partisan power, the Chinese became a political issue. This was the greatest evil that could befall them, for now racial persecution received official sanction and passed out of the hands of mere ruffians into the custody of powerful political agitators. Under the lurid leadership of Dennis Kearney, the Workingman's party was organized for the purpose of influencing legislation and "ridding the country of Chinese cheap labor." Their goal was "Four dollars a day and roast beef"; and their battle cry, "The Chinese must go." Under the excitement of sand-lot meetings, the Chinese were driven under cover. In the riots of July, 1877, in San Francisco, twenty-five Chinese laundries were burned. "For months afterward," says Mary Roberts Coolidge, "no Chinaman was safe from personal outrage even on the main thoroughfares, and the perpetrators of the abuses were almost never interfered with so long as they did not molest white men's property."[1]

This anti-Chinese epidemic soon spread to other Western States. Legislatures and city councils vied with each other in passing laws and ordinances to satisfy the demands of the labor vote. All manner of ingenious devices were incorporated into tax laws in an endeavor to drive the Chinese out of certain occupations and to exclude them from the State. License and occupation taxes multiplied. The Chinaman was denied the privilege of citizenship, was excluded from the public schools, and was not allowed to give testimony in proceedings relating to white persons. Manifold ordinances were passed intended to harass and humiliate him: for instance, a San Francisco ordinance required the hair of all prisoners to be cut within three inches of the scalp. Most extreme and unreasonable discriminations against hand laundries were framed. The new California constitution of 1879 endowed the legislature and the cities with large powers in regulating the conditions under which Chinese would be tolerated. In 1880 a state law declared that all corporations operating under a state charter should be prohibited from employing

[1] *Chinese Immigration*, p. 265.

Chinese under penalty of forfeiting their charter. Chinese were also excluded from employment in all public works. Nearly all these laws and ordinances, however, were ultimately declared to be unconstitutional on account of their discriminatory character or because they were illegal regulations of commerce.

The States having failed to exclude the Chinese, the only hope left was in the action of the Federal Government. The earliest treaties and trade conventions with China (1844 and 1858) had been silent upon the rights and privileges of Chinese residing or trading in the United States. In 1868, Anson Burlingame, who had served for six years as American Minister to China, but who had now entered the employ of the Chinese Imperial Government, arrived at the head of a Chinese mission sent for the purpose of negotiating a new treaty which should insure reciprocal rights to the Chinese. The journey from San Francisco to Washington was a sort of triumphal progress and everywhere the Chinese mission was received with acclaim. The treaty drawn by Secretary Seward was ratified on July 28, 1868, and was hailed even on the Pacific coast as the beginning of more fortunate relations between the two countries. The treaty acknowledged the "inherent and inalienable right of man to change his home and allegiance, and also the mutual advantage of the free migration and emigration of their citizens and subjects respectively, from the one country to the other, for purposes of curiosity, of trade or as permanent residents." It stated positively that "citizens of the United States visiting or residing in China shall enjoy the same privileges, immunities, and exemptions in respect to travel and residence as may be enjoyed by the citizens of the most favored nation. And, reciprocally, Chinese subjects visiting or residing in the United States shall enjoy the same privileges, immunities, and exemptions in respect to travel or residence." The right to naturalization was by express statement not conferred by the treaty upon the subjects of either nation dwelling in the territory of the other. But it was not in any way prohibited.

The applause which greeted this international agreement had hardly subsided before the anti-Chinese agitators discovered that the treaty was in their way and they thereupon demanded its modification or abrogation. They now raised the cry that the Chinese were a threat to the morals and health of the country, that the majority of

Chinese immigrants were either coolies under contract, criminals, diseased persons, or prostitutes. As a result, in 1879 a representative from Nevada, one of the States particularly interested, introduced in Congress a bill limiting to fifteen the Chinese passengers that any ship might bring to the United States on a single voyage, and requiring the captains of such vessels to register at the port of entry a list of their Chinese passengers. The Senate added an amendment requesting the President to notify the Chinese Government that the section of the Burlingame treaty insuring reciprocal interchange of citizens was abrogated. After a very brief debate the measure that so flagrantly defied an international treaty passed both houses. It was promptly vetoed, however, by President Hayes on the ground that it violated a treaty which a friendly nation had carefully observed. If the Pacific cities had cause of complaint, the President preferred to remedy the situation by the "proper course of diplomatic negotiations."[1]

[1] So intense was the feeling in the West that at this time a letter purporting to have been written by James A. Garfield, the Republican candidate, favoring unrestricted immigration, was published on the eve of the Presidential election (1880). Though the letter was shown to be a forgery, yet it was not without influence. In California Garfield received only one of the six electoral votes; and in Nevada he received none. In Denver,

The President accordingly appointed a commission, under the chairmanship of James B. Angell, president of the University of Michigan, to negotiate a new treaty. The commission proceeded to China and completed its task in November, 1880. The new treaty provided that, "whenever, in the opinion of the Government of the United States, the coming of Chinese laborers to the United States, or their residence therein, affects or threatens to affect the interests of that country, or to endanger the good order of the said country or of any locality within the territory thereof, the Government of China agrees that the Government of the United States may regulate, limit, or suspend such coming or residence, but may not absolutely prohibit it." Other Chinese subjects who had come to the United States, "as travelers, merchants, or for curiosity," and laborers already in the United States, were to "be allowed to go and come of their own free will," with all of the "rights, privileges, immunities, and exemptions which are accorded to the citizens of the most favored nation." The United States furthermore undertook

---

where only four hundred Chinese lived, race riots occurred which cost one Chinaman his life and destroyed Chinese property to the amount of $50,000.

to protect the Chinese in the United States against "ill treatment" and to "devise means for their protection."

Two years after the ratification of this treaty, a bill was introduced to prohibit the immigration of Chinese labor for twenty years. Both the great political parties had included the subject in their platforms in 1880. The Democrats had espoused exclusion and were committed to "No more Chinese immigration"; the Republicans had preferred restriction by "just, humane, and reasonable laws." The bill passed, but President Arthur vetoed it on the ground that prohibiting immigration for so long a period transcended the provisions of the treaty. A bill which was then passed shortening the period of the restriction to ten years received the President's signature, and on August 5, 1882, America shut the door in the face of Chinese labor.

The law, however, was very loosely drawn and administrative confusion arose at once. Chinese laborers leaving the United States were required to obtain a certificate from the collector of customs at the port of departure entitling them to reëntry. Other Chinese — merchants, travelers, or visitors — who desired to come to the United States were required to have a certificate from their Government declaring that they were entitled to enter under the provisions of the treaty. As time went on, identification became a joke, trading in certificates a regular pursuit, and smuggling Chinese across the Canadian border a profitable business. Moreover, in the light of the law, who was a "merchant" and who a "visitor"? In 1884 Congress attempted to remedy these defects of phraseology and administration by carefully framed definitions and stringent measures.[1] The Supreme Court upheld the constitutionality of exclusion as incident to American sovereignty.

Meanwhile in the West the popular feeling against the Chinese refused to subside. At Rock Springs, Wyoming, twenty-eight Chinese were killed and fifteen were injured by a mob which also destroyed Chinese property amounting to $148,000. At Tacoma and Seattle, also, violence descended upon the Mongolian. In San Francisco a special grand jury which investigated the operation of the exclusion laws and a committee of the Board of Supervisors which investigated the condition of Chinatown both made reports that were violently anti-Chinese. A state anti-Chinese convention

[1] Wong Wing vs. U. S., 163 U. S. 235.

soon thereafter declared that the situation "had become well-nigh intolerable." So widespread and venomous was the agitation against Chinese that President Cleveland was impelled to send to Congress two special messages on the question, detailing the facts and requesting Congress to pay the Chinese claims for indemnity which Wyoming refused to honor. The remonstrances of the Chinese Government led to the drafting of a new treaty in 1888. But while China was deliberating over this treaty, Congress summarily shut off any hope for immediate agreement by passing the Scott Act prohibiting the return of any Chinese laborer after the passage of the act, stopping the issue of any more certificates of identification, and declaring void all certificates previously issued. It is difficult to avoid the conclusion that this brutal political measure was passed with an eye to the Pacific electoral vote in the pending election. In the next presidential year the climax of harshness was reached in the Geary law, which required, within an unreasonably short time, the registration of all Chinese in the United States. The Chinese, under legal advice, refused to register until the Federal Supreme Court had declared the law constitutional. Subsequently the time for registration was extended.

The anti-Chinese fanaticism had now reached its highest point. While the Government maintained its policy of exclusion, it modified the drastic details of the law. In 1894 a new treaty provided for the exclusion of laborers for ten years, excepting registered laborers who had either parent, wife, or child in the United States, or who possessed property or debts to the amount of one thousand dollars. It required all resident Chinese laborers to register, and the Chinese Government was similarly entitled to require the registration of all American laborers resident in China. The treaty made optional the clause requiring merchants, travelers, and other classes privileged to come to the United States, to secure a certificate from their Government viséd by the American representative at the port of departure.

In 1898 General Otis extended the exclusion acts to the Philippines by military order, owing to the fact that the country was in a state of war, and Congress extended them to the Hawaiian Islands. In 1904 China refused to continue the treaty of 1894, and Congress substantially reënacted the existing laws "in so far as not inconsistent with treaty obligations." Thus the legal *status quo* has been maintained, and the Chinese population in

America is gradually decreasing. No new laborers are permitted to come and those now here go home as old age overtakes them. But the public has come to recognize that diplomatic circumlocution cannot conceal the crude and harsh treatment which the Chinaman has received; that the earlier laws were based upon reports that greatly exaggerated the evils and were silent upon the virtues of the Oriental; and that a policy which had its conception in frontier fears and in race prejudice was sustained by politicians and perpetuated by demagogues.

Rather suddenly the whole drama of discrimination was re-opened by the arrival of a considerable number of Japanese laborers in America. In 1900, there were some twenty-four thousand in the United States and a decade later this number had increased threefold. About one-half of them lived in California, and the rest were to be found throughout the West, especially in Washington, Colorado, and Oregon. They were nearly all unmarried young men of the peasant class. Unlike the Chinese, they manifested a readiness to conform to American customs and an eagerness to learn the language and to adopt American dress. The racial gulf, however, is not bridged by a similarity in externals. The Japanese possess all the deep and subtle contrasts of mentality and ideality which differentiate the Orient from the Occident. A few are not averse to adopting Christianity; many more are free-thinkers; but the bulk remain loyal to Buddhism. They have reproduced here the compact trade guilds of Japan. The persistent aggressiveness of the Japanese, their cunning, their aptitude in taking advantage of critical circumstances in making bargains, have by contrast partially restored to popular favor the patient, reliable Chinaman.

At first the Japanese were welcomed as unskilled laborers. They found employment on the railroads, in lumber mills and salmon canneries, in mines and on farms, and in domestic service. But they soon showed a keen propensity for owning or leasing land. The Immigration Commission found that in 1909 they owned over sixteen thousand acres in California and leased over one hundred and thirty-seven thousand. Nearly all of this land they had acquired in the preceding five years. In Colorado they controlled over twenty thousand acres, and in Idaho and Washington over seven thousand acres each. This acreage represents small holdings devoted to intensive agriculture, especially to the raising of sugar beets, vegetables, and small fruits.

The hostility which began to manifest itself against the Japanese especially in California brought that State into sharp contact with the Federal Government. In 1906 the San Francisco authorities excluded the Japanese from the public schools. This act was immediately and vigorously protested by the Japanese Government. After due investigation, the matter was finally adjusted at a conference held in Washington between President Roosevelt and a delegation from California. This incident served to re-awaken the ghost of Mongolian domination on the Pacific coast, for it occurred during the notorious régime of Mayor Schmitz. Labor politics were rampant. Isolated instances of violence against Japanese occurred, and hoodlums, without fear of police interference, attacked a number of Japanese restaurants. Political candidates were pledged to an anti-Japanese policy.

In 1907 the two governments reached an agreement whereby the details of issuing passports to Japanese laborers who desired to return to the United States was virtually left in the hands of the Japanese Government, which was opposed to the emigration of its laboring population. As a consequence of this agreement, passports are granted only to laborers who had previously been residents of the United States or to parents, wives, and children of Japanese laborers resident in America. Under authority of the immigration law of 1907, the President issued an order (March 14, 1907) denying admission to "Japanese and Korean laborers, skilled or unskilled, who have received passports to go to Mexico, Canada, Hawaii and come therefrom" to the United States.

Anti-Japanese feeling was crystallized into the alien land bill of California in 1913. So serious was the international situation that President Wilson sent Mr. Bryan, then Secretary of State, across the continent to confer with the California legislature and to determine upon some action that would at the same time meet the needs of the State and "leave untouched the international obligations of the United States." The law subsequently passed was thought by the Californians to appease both of these demands. [1] But the Japanese Government made no less than five vigorous formal protests

[1] The Alien Land Act of May 19, 1913, confers upon all aliens eligible to citizenship the same rights as citizens in the owning and leasing of real property; but in the case of other aliens (*i.e.* Asiatics) it limits leases of land for agricultural purposes to terms not exceeding three years and permits ownership "to the extent and for the purposes prescribed by any treaty."

and filled a lengthy brief which characterized the law as unfair and intentionally discriminating and in violation of the treaty of Commerce and Navigation entered into in 1911. While anti-Japanese demonstrations were taking place in Washington, there was a corresponding outbreak of anti-American feeling in the streets of Tokyo. On February 2, 1914, during the debate on a new immigration bill, an amendment was proposed in the House of Representatives, at the instigation of members from the Pacific coast, excluding all Asiatics, except such as had their entry right established by treaty. But this drastic proposal was defeated by a decisive vote.

The oriental question in America is further complicated by the fact that since 1905 some five thousand East Indians have come to the United States. Of these the majority are Hindoos, the remainder being chiefly Afghans. How these people who have lived under British rule will adapt themselves to American life and institutions remains to be seen.

CHAPTER X

With the free land gone and the cities crowded to overflowing, the door of immigration, though guarded, nevertheless remains open and the pressure of the old-world peoples continues. Where can they go? They are filling in the vacant spots of the older States, the abandoned farms, stagnant half-empty villages, undrained swamps, uninviting rocky hillsides. This infiltration of foreigners possessing themselves of rejected and abandoned land, which has only recently begun, shows that the peasant's instinct for the soil will reassert itself when the means are available and the way opens.

It is surprising, indeed, how many are the ways that are opening for this movement. Transportation companies are responsible for a number of colonies planted bodily in cut-over timber regions of the South. The journals and the real estate agents of the different races are always alert to spy out opportunities. Dealing in second-hand farms has become a considerable industry. The advertising columns of Chicago papers announce hundreds of farms for sale in northern Michigan and Wisconsin. In all the older States there are for sale thousands of acres of tillable land which have been left by the restless shiftings of the American population. In New England the abandoned farm has long been an institution. Throughout the East there are depleted and dying villages, their solidly built cottages hidden in the matting of trees and shrubs which neglect has woven about them. One can see paralysis creeping over them as the vines creep over their deserted thresholds and they surrender one by one the little industries that gave them life.

These are the opportunities of the immigrant peasant. Wherever the new migration swarms, there the receding tide leaves a few energetic individuals who have made for themselves a permanent home. In the wake of construction gangs and along the lines of railways and canals one discovers these immigrant families taking root in the soil. In the smaller cities, an immigrant day laborer will often invest his savings in a tumble-down house and an acre of land, and almost at once he becomes the nucleus for a gathering of his kind.

The market gardens that surround the large cities offer work to the children of the factory operatives, and there they swarm over beet and onion fields like huge insects with an unerring instinct for weeds. Now and then a family finds a forgotten acre, builds a shack, and starts a small independent market garden. Within a few years a whole settlement of shacks grows up around it, and soon the trucking of the neighborhood is in foreign hands. Seasonal agricultural work often carries the immigrant into distant canning centers, hop fields, cranberry marshes, orchards, and vineyards. Every time a migration of this sort occurs, some settlers remain on land previously thought unfit for cultivation — perhaps a swamp which they drain or a sand-hill which they fertilize and nurture into surprising fertility by constant toil. This racial seepage is confined almost wholly to the Italian and the Slav.

There is a vast acreage of unoccupied good land in the South, which the negro, usually satisfied with a bare living, has neither the enterprise nor the thrift to cultivate. The prejudice of the former slave owner against the foreign immigration for many years retarded the development of this land. About 1880, however, groups of Italians, attracted by the sunny climate and the opportunities for making a livelihood, began to seep into Louisiana. By 1900 they numbered over seventeen thousand. When direct sailings between the Mediterranean and the Gulf of Mexico were established, their numbers increased rapidly and New Orleans became one of the leading Italian centers in the United States. From the city they soon spread into the adjoining region. Today they grow cotton, sugarcane, and rice in nearly all the Southern States. In the deep black loam of the Yazoo Delta they prosper as cotton growers. They have transformed the neglected slopes of the Ozarks into apple and peach orchards. New Orleans, Dallas, Galveston, Houston, San Antonio, and other Southern cities are supplied with vegetables from the Italian truck farms. At Independence, Louisiana, a colony raises strawberries. In the black belt of Arkansas they established Sunnyside in 1895, a colony which has survived many vicissitudes and has been the parent of other similar enterprises. In Texas there are a number of such colonies, of which the largest, at Bryan, numbers nearly two thousand persons. In California the Italian owns farms, orchards, vineyards, market gardens, and even ranches. Here he finds the cloudless sky and mild air of his native land. The sunny slopes invite vine culture.

In the North and the East the alert Italian has found many opportunities to buy land. In the environs of nearly every city northward from Norfolk, Virginia, are to be found his truck patches. At Vineland and Hammonton, New Jersey, large colonies have flourished for many years. In New York and Pennsylvania, many a hill farm that was too rocky for its Yankee owner, and many a back-breaking clay moraine in Ohio and Indiana has been purchased for a small cash payment and, under the stimulus of the family's coaxing, now yields paying crops, while the father himself also earns a daily wage in the neighboring town. Where one such Italian family is to be found, there are sure to be found at least two or three others in the neighborhood, for the Italians hate isolation more than hunger. Often they are clustered in colonies, as at Genoa and Cumberland in Wisconsin, where most of them are railroad workmen paying for the land out of their wages.

The Slavs, too, wedge into the most surprising spaces. Their colonies and settlements are to be found in considerable numbers in every part of the Union except the far South. They are on the cut-over timber lands of Michigan, Wisconsin, and Minnesota, usually engaged in dairying or raising

vegetables for canning. On the great prairies in
Iowa, Nebraska, Kansas, and the Dakotas, the
Bohemians and the Poles have learned to raise
wheat and corn, and in Texas, Oklahoma, and Arkansas, they have shown themselves skillful in
cotton raising. Wherever fruit is grown on the Pacific slope, there are Bohemians, Slavonians, and
Dalmatians. In New England, Ohio, Illinois, Indiana, and Maryland, the Poles have become pioneers in the neglected corners of the land. For
instance in Orange County, New York, a thriving
settlement from old Poland now flourishes where
a quarter of a century ago there was only a mos-
quito breeding swamp. The drained area pro-
duces the most surprising crops of onions, lettuce,
and celery. Many of these immigrants own their
little farms. Others work on shares in anticipa-
tion of ownership, and still others labor merely
for the season, transients who spend the winter
either in American factories or flit back to their
native land.

In Pennsylvania it is the mining towns which
furnished recruits for this landward movement. In
some of the counties an exchange of population has
been taking place for a decade or more. The land
dwelling Americans are moving into the towns and

cities. The farms are offered for sale. Enterpris-
ing Slavic real estate dealers are not slow in per-
suading their fellow countrymen to invest their
savings in land.

The Slavonic infiltration has been most marked
in New England, especially in the Connecticut Valley. From manufacturing centers like Chicopee,
Worcester, Ware, Westfield, and Fitchburg, areas
of Polish settlements radiate in every direction,
alien spokes from American hubs. Here are little
farming villages ready made in attractive settings
whose vacant houses invite the alien peasant. A
Polish family moves into a sedate colonial house;
often a second family shares the place, sometimes
a third or a fourth, each with a brood of children
and often a boarder or two. The American families left in the neighborhood are scandalized by
this promiscuity, by the bare feet and bare heads,
by the unspeakable fare, the superstition and credulity, and illiteracy and disregard for sanitary
measures, and by the ant-like industry from starlight to starlight. Old Hadley has become a pro-
totype of what may become general if this racial
infiltration is not soon checked. In 1906 the Poles
numbered one-fifth of the population in that town,
owned one-twentieth of the land, and produced

two-thirds of the babies. Dignified old streets that formerly echoed with the tread of patriots now resound to the din of Polish weddings and christenings, and the town that sheltered William Goffe, one of the judges before whom Charles I was tried, now houses Polish transients at twenty-five cents a bed weekly.

The transient usually returns to Europe, but the landowner remains. His kind is increasing yearly. It is even probable that in a generation he will be the chief landowner of the Connecticut Valley. It will take more than an association of old families, determined on keeping the ancient homes in their own hands, to check this transformation.

The process of racial replacement is most rapid in the smaller manufacturing towns. In the New England mills the Yankee gave way to the Irish, the Irish gave way to the French Canadian, and the French Canadian has been largely superseded by the Slav and the Italian. Every one of the older industrial towns has been encrusted in layer upon layer of foreign accretions, until it is difficult to discover the American core. Everywhere are the physiognomy, the chatter, and the aroma of the modern steerage. Lawrence, Massachusetts, is typical of this change. In 1848 it had 5923 inhabitants, of whom 63.3 per cent were Americans, 36 per cent were Irish, and about forty white persons belonged to other nationalities. In 1910 the same city had 85,000 inhabitants, of whom only about 14 per cent were Americans, and the rest foreigners, two-thirds of the old and one-third of the new immigration.

A like transformation has taken place in the manufacturing towns of New York, New Jersey, and Delaware and in the iron and steel towns of Pennsylvania, West Virginia, and the Middle West. For forty years after the establishment of the first iron furnace in Johnstown, Pennsylvania, in 1842, the mills were manned exclusively by Americans, English, Welsh, Irish, and Germans. In 1880 Slavic names began to appear on the pay rolls. Soon thereafter Italians and Syrians were brought into the town, and today sixty per cent of the population is of foreign birth, largely from southeastern Europe. The native Americans and Welsh live in two wards, and clustered around them are settlements of Italians, Slovaks, and Croatians.

The new manufacturing towns which are dependent upon some single industry are almost wholly composed of recent immigrants. Gary, Indiana,

built by the United States Steel Corporation, and
Whiting, Indiana, established by the Standard Oil
Company for its refining industry, are examples of
new American towns of exotic populations. At a
glass factory built in 1890 in the village of Charleroi,
Pennsylvania, over ten thousand Belgians, French,
Slavs, and Italians now labor. An example of
lightning-like displacement of population is afforded by the steel and iron center at Granite City
and Madison, Illinois. The two towns are prac-
tically one industrial community, although they
have separate municipal organizations. A steel mill
was erected in 1892 upon the open prairies, and
in it American, Welsh, Irish, English, German, and
Polish workmen were employed. In 1900 Slovaks
were brought in, and two years later there came
large numbers of Magyars, followed by Croatians.
In 1905 Bulgarians began to arrive, and within two
years over eight thousand had assembled. Armenians, Servians, Greeks, Magyars, every ethnic faction found in the racial welter of southeastern Europe, is represented among the twenty thousand inhabitants that dwell in this new industrial town.
In "Hungary Hollow" these race fragments iso-
late themselves, effectively insulated against the
currents of American influence.

The mining communities reveal this relative displacement of races in its most disheartening form. As early as 1820 coal was taken from the anthracite veins of northeastern Pennsylvania, but until 1880 the industry was dominated by Americans and north Europeans. In 1870 out of 108,000 foreign born in this region, 105,000 or over ninety-seven per cent came from England, Wales, Scotland, Ireland, and Germany. In 1880 a change began and continued until in 1910 less than one-third of the 267,000 foreign born were of northern European extraction. In 1870 there were only 306 Slavs and Italians in the entire region; in 1890 there were 43,000; in 1909 there were 89,000; and in 1910 the number increased to 178,000.

Today these immigrants from the south of Europe have virtually displaced the miner from the north. They have rooted out the decencies and comforts of the earlier operatives and have supplanted them with the promiscuity, the filth, and the low economic standards of the medieval peasant. There are no more desolate and distressing places in America than the miserable mining "patches" clinging like lichens to the steep hillsides or secluded in the valleys of Pennsylvania. In the bituminous fields conditions are no better.

In the town of Windber in western Pennsylvania, for example, some two thousand experienced English and American miners were engaged in opening the veins in 1897. No sooner were the mines in operation than the south European began to drift in. Today he outnumbers and underbids the American and the north European. He lives in isolated sections, reeking with everything that keeps him a "foreigner" in the heart of America. The coal regions of Virginia, West Virginia, Ohio, Indiana, and Illinois and the ore regions of northern Michigan and Minnesota are rapidly passing under the same influence.

Every mining and manufacturing community is thus an ethnic pool, whence little streams of foreigners trickle over the land. These isolated miners and tillers of the soil are more immune to American ideals than are their city dwelling brethren. They are not jostled and shaken by other races; no mental contagion of democracy reaches them.

But within the towns and cities another process of replacement is going on. Its index is written large in the signs over shops and stores and clearly in the lists of professional men in the city directories and in the pay roll of the public school teachers. The unpronounceable Slavic combinations of consonants and polysyllabic Jewish patronymics are plentiful, while here and there an Italian name makes its appearance. The second generation is arriving. The sons and daughters are leaving the factory and the construction gang for the counter, the office, and the schoolroom.

American ideals and institutions have borne and can bear a great deal of foreign infiltration. But can they withstand saturation?

CHAPTER XI

"WHOSOEVER will may come" was the generous welcome which America extended to all the world for over a century. Many alarms, indeed, there were and several well-defined movements to save America from the foreigner. The first of these attempts resulted in the ill-fated Alien and Sedition laws of 1798, which extended to fourteen years the period of probation before a foreigner could be naturalized and which attempted to safeguard the Government against defamatory attacks. The Jeffersonians, who came into power in 1801 largely upon the issue raised by this attempt to curtail free speech, made short shrift of this unpopular law and restored the term of residence to five years. The second anti-foreign movement found expression in the Know-Nothing party, which rose in the decade preceding the Civil War. The third movement brought about a secret order called the American

Protective Association, popularly known as the A. P. A., which, like the Know-Nothing hysteria, was aimed primarily at the Catholic Church. Its platform stated that "the conditions growing out of our immigration laws are such as to weaken our democratic institutions," and that "the immigrant vote, under the direction of certain ecclesiastical institutions," controlled politics. In 1896 the organization claimed two and a half million adherents, and the air was vibrant with ominous rumors of impending events. But nothing happened. The A. P. A. disappeared suddenly and left no trace.

For over a century it was almost universally believed that the prosperity of the country depended largely upon a copious influx of population. This sentiment found expression in President Lincoln's message to Congress on December 8, 1863, in which he called immigration a "source of national wealth and strength" and urged Congress to establish "a system for the encouragement of immigration." In conformity with this suggestion, Congress passed a law designed to aid the importation of labor under contract. But the measure was soon repealed, so that it remains the only instance in American history in which the Federal

Government attempted the direct encouragement of general immigration.[1]

It was in 1819 that the first Federal law pertaining to immigration was passed. It was not prompted by any desire to regulate or restrict immigration, but aimed rather to correct the terrible abuses to which immigrants were subject on shipboard. So crowded and unwholesome were these quarters that a substantial percentage of all the immigrants who embarked for America perished during the voyage. The law provided that ships could carry only two passengers for every five tons burden; it enjoined a sufficient supply of water and food for crew and passengers; and it required the captains of vessels to prepare lists of their passengers giving age, sex, occupation, and the country whence they came. The law, however good its intention, was loosely drawn and indifferently enforced. Terrible abuses of steerage passengers crowded into miserable quarters were constantly brought to the public notice. From time to time the law was amended, and the advent of steam navigation brought improved conditions without, however, adequate provision for Federal inspection.

[1] Congress has on several occasions granted aid for specific colonies or groups of immigrants.

Indeed such supervision and care as immigrants received was provided by the various States. Boston, New York, Baltimore, and other ports of entry, found helpless hordes left at their doors. They were the prey of loan sharks and land sharks, of fake employment agencies, and every conceivable form of swindler. Private relief was organized, but it could reach only a small portion of the needy. About three-fourths of the immigrants disembarked at the port of New York, and upon the State of New York was imposed the obligation of looking after the thousands of strangers who landed weekly at the Battery. To cope with these conditions the State devised a comprehensive system and entrusted its enforcement to a Board of Commissioners of Immigration, erected hospitals on Ward's Island for sick and needy immigrants, and in 1855 leased for a landing place Castle Garden, which at once became the popular synonym for the nation's gateway. Here the Commissioners examined and registered the immigrants, placed at their disposal physicians, money changers, transportation agents, and advisers, and extended to them a helping hand. The Federal Government was represented only by the customs officers who ransacked their baggage.

In 1875 the Federal Supreme Court decided that it was unconstitutional for a State to regulate immigration. "We are of the opinion," said the Court, "that this whole subject has been confided to Congress by the Constitution; that Congress can more appropriately and with more acceptance exercise it than any other body known to our law, state or national; that, by providing a system of laws in these matters applicable to all ports and to all vessels, a serious question which has long been a matter of contest and complaint may be effectively and satisfactorily settled."[1] Congress dallied seven years with this important question, and was finally forced to act when New York threatened to close Castle Garden. In 1882 a Federal immigration law assessed a head tax of fifty cents on every passenger, not a citizen, coming to the United States, and provided that the States should share with the Secretary of the Treasury the obligation of its enforcement. This law inaugurated the policy of selective immigration, as it excluded convicts, lunatics, idiots, and persons likely to become a public charge. Three years later, contract laborers were also excluded.

[1] Henderson et al. *vs.* The Mayor of New York City et al. 92 U.S., 259.

The unprecedented influx of immigrants now began to arouse public discussion. Over 788,000 arrived in America during the first year the new law was in operation. In 1889 both the Senate and the House appointed standing committees on immigration. The several investigations which were held culminated in the law of 1891, wherein the list of ineligibles was extended to include persons suffering from a loathsome or contagious disease, polygamists, and persons assisted in coming by others, unless upon special inquiry they were found not to belong to any of the excluded classes. Thus for the first time the Federal Government assumed complete control of immigration. Now also both the great political parties adopted planks in their national platforms favoring the restriction of immigration. The Republicans favored "the enactment of more stringent laws and regulations for the restriction of criminal, pauper, and contract immigration." The Democrats "heartily" approved "all legislative efforts to prevent the United States from being used as a dumping ground for the known criminals and professional paupers of Europe," and they favored the exclusion of Chinese laborers. They favored, however, the admission of "industrious and worthy" Europeans.

Selective immigration thus became a political issue in 1892, partly under the stimulus of labor unions, which feared an over-supply of labor, and partly because of the growing popular belief that many undesirable foreigners were entering the country. No adequate and just criteria for any process of selection have been discovered. In 1896 Senator Lodge introduced an immigration bill, which contained the famous literacy test, excluding all persons between fourteen and sixty years of age "who cannot both read and write the English language or some other language." The bill was simultaneously introduced into the House of Representatives by McCall of Massachusetts. The debate on this measure marks a new departure in immigration policy. A senatorial inquiry made among the States in the preceding year had disclosed a universal preference for immigrants from northern Europe. Moreover, a number of States through their governors, had declared that further immigration was not desired immediately; and the opinion prevailed that the great influx from southeastern Europe should be checked. Fortified by such solidarity of sentiment, Congress passed the Lodge bill with certain amendments. President Cleveland, however, returned it with a strong veto message on March 2, 1897. He could not concur in so radical a departure from the traditional liberal policy of the Government; and he believed the literacy test so artificial that it was more rational "to admit a hundred thousand immigrants who, though unable to read and write, seek among us only a home and opportunity to work, than to admit one of those unruly agitators and enemies of governmental control who can not only read and write, but delights in arousing by inflammatory speech the illiterate and peacefully inclined to discontent and tumult." The House passed the bill over the President's veto, but the Senate took no further action.

In 1898 the Industrial Commission was empowered "to investigate questions pertaining to immigration" and presented a report which prepared the way for the immigration law of 1903, approved on the 3rd of March. This law, which was based upon a careful preliminary inquiry, may be called the first comprehensive American immigration statute. It perfected the administrative machinery, raised the head tax, and multiplied the vigilance of the Government against evasions by the excluded classes. Anarchists and prostitutes were added to the list of excluded persons. The literacy test was inserted by the House but was rejected by the Senate.

This law, however, did not allay the demand for a more stringent restriction of immigration. A few persons believed in stopping immigration entirely for a period of years. Others would limit the number of immigrants that should be permitted to enter every year. But it was felt throughout the country that such arbitrary checks would be merely quantitative, not qualitative, and that undesirable foreigners should be denied admission, no matter what country they hailed from. A notable immigration conference which was called by the National Civic Federation in December, 1905, and which represented all manner of public bodies, recommended the "exclusion of persons of enfeebled vitality" and proposed "a preliminary inspection of intending immigrants before they embark." President Roosevelt laid the whole matter before Congress in several vigorous messages in 1906 and 1907. He pointed to the fact that

In the year ending June 30, 1905, there came to the United States 1,026,000 alien immigrants. In other words, in the single year . . . there came . . . a greater number of people than came here during the one hundred and sixty-nine years of our colonial life.

. . . It is clearly shown in the report of the Commissioner General of Immigration that, while much of this enormous immigration is undoubtedly healthy and natural . . . a considerable proportion of it, probably a very large proportion, including most of the undesirable class, does not come here of its own initiative but because of the activity of the agents of the great transportation companies. . . . The prime need is to keep out all immigrants who will not make good American citizens.

In consonance with this spirit, the law of 1907 was passed. It increased the head tax to four dollars and provided rigid scrutiny over the transportation companies. The excluded classes of immigrants were minutely defined, and the powers and duties of the Commissioner General of Immigration were very considerably enlarged. The act also created the Immigration Commission, consisting of three Senators, three members of the House, and three persons appointed by the President, for making "full inquiry, examination, and investigation . . . into the subject of immigration." Endowed with plenary power, this commission made a comprehensive investigation of the whole question. The President was authorized to "send special commissioners to any foreign country for the purpose of regulating by international agreement . . . the immigration of aliens to the United States."

Here at last is congressional recognition of the fact that immigration is no longer merely a domestic question, but that it has, through modern economic conditions, become one of serious international import. No treaties have been perfected under this authority. The question, however, received serious attention in 1909 when Lieutenant Joseph Petrosino of the New York police was murdered in Sicily by banditti, whither he had pursued a Black Hand criminal from the East Side.

In the meantime many measures for restricting immigration were suggested in Congress. Of these, the literacy test met with the most favor. Three times in recent years Congress enacted it into law, and each time it was returned with executive disapproval: President Taft vetoed the provision in 1913, and President Wilson vetoed the acts of 1915 and 1917. In his last veto message on January 29, 1917, President Wilson said that "the literacy test . . . is not a test of character, of quality, or of personal fitness, but would operate in most cases merely as a penalty for lack of opportunity in the country from which the alien seeking admission came."

Congress, however, promptly passed the bill over the President's objections, and so twenty years after President Cleveland's veto of the Lodge Bill, the literacy test became the standard of fitness for immigrant admission into the United States.[1] The law excludes all aliens over sixteen years of age who are physically capable of reading and yet who cannot read. They are required to read "not less than thirty or more than eighty words in ordinary use" in the English language or some other language or dialect. Aliens who seek admission because of religious persecution, and certain relatives of citizens or of admissible aliens, are exempted.

The debate upon this law disclosed the transformation that has come over the nation in its attitude towards the alien. Exclusion was the dominant word. Senator Reed of Missouri wished to exclude African immigrants; the Pacific coast Representatives insisted upon exclusion of Asiatics, in the face of serious admonitions of the Secretary of State that such a course would cause international friction; the labor members were scornful in their denunciation of "the pauper and criminal classes" of Europe. The traditional liberal sympathies of the American people found but few

[1] The new act took effect May 1, 1917.

champions, so completely had the change been wrought in the thirty years since the Federal Government assumed control of immigration.

By these tokens the days of unlimited freedom in migration are numbered. Nations are beginning to realize that immigration is but the obverse of emigration. Its dual character constitutes a problem requiring delicate international readjustments. Moreover, the countries released to a new life and those quickened to a new industrialism by the Great War will need to employ all their muscle and talents at home.

It is an inspiring drama of colonization that has been enacted on this continent in a relatively short period. Its like was never witnessed before and can never be witnessed again. Thirty-three nationalities were represented in the significant group of American pilgrims that gathered at Mount Vernon on July 4, 1918, to place garlands of native flowers upon the tomb of Washington and to pledge their honor and loyalty to the nation of their adoption. This event is symbolic of the great fact that the United States is, after all, a nation of immigrants, among whom the word foreigner is descriptive of an attitude of mind rather than of a place of birth.

BIBLIOGRAPHICAL NOTE

GENERAL HISTORIES

EDWARD CHANNING, *History of the United States*, 4 vols. (1905). Vol. II. Chapter XIV contains a fascinating account of "The Coming of the Foreigner."

John Fiske, *Dutch and Quaker Colonies in America*, 2 vols. (1899). The story of "The Migration of the Sects" is charmingly told.

John B. McMaster, *History of the People of the United States*, 8 vols. (1883–1913). Scattered throughout the eight volumes are copious accounts of the coming of immigrants, from the year of American independence to the Civil War. The great German and Irish inundations are dealt with in volumes VI and VII.

J. H. Latané, *America as a World Power* (1907). Chapter XVII gives a concise summary of immigration for the years 1880–1907.

WORKS ON IMMIGRATION

Reports of the Immigration Commission, appointed under the Congressional Act of Feb. 20, 1907. 42 vols. (1911). This is by far the most exhaustive study that has been made of the immigration question. It embraces a wide range of details, especially upon the economic and sociological aspects of the problem.

Census Bureau, *A Century of Population Growth from the First Census of the United States to the Twelfth, 1790–1900* (1909). The best analysis of the population of the United States. It contains a number of chapters on the population at the time of the First Census in 1790.

John R. Commons, *Races and Immigrants in America* (1907).

Prescott F. Hall, *Immigration and its Effects upon the United States* (1906).

Henry P. Fairchild, *Immigration, a World Movement and its American Significance* (1913). A good historical survey of immigration as well as a suggestive discussion of its sociological and economic bearings.

Jeremiah W. Jenks and W. Jett Lauck, *The Immigration Problem* (1913). A summary of the Report of the Immigration Commission.

Peter Roberts, *The New Immigration* (1912). A discussion of the recent influx from Southeastern Europe.

E. A. Ross, *The Old World in the New* (1914) contains some refreshing racial characteristics.

Richmond Mayo-Smith, *Emigration and Immigration* (1890). This is one of the oldest American works on the subject and remains the best scientific discussion of the sociological and economic aspects of immigration.

Edward A. Steiner, *On the Trail of the Immigrant* (1906). A popular and sympathetic account of the new immigration.

THE NEGRO

B. G. Brawley, *A Short History of the American Negro* (1913).

W. E. B. Du Bois, *The Negro* (1915). A small well-written volume, with a useful bibliography and an illuminating chapter on the negro in the United States; also, by the same author, *Suppression of the African Slave Trade* (1896).

Carter G. Woodson, *A Century of Negro Migration* (1918).

J. R. Spears, *The American Slave Trade* (1900).

A. H. Stone, *Studies in the American Race Problem* (1908). Contains several of Walter F. Wilcox's valuable statistical studies on this subject.

J. A. Tillinghast, *The Negro in Africa and America* (1902) contains a suggestive comparison of negro life in Africa and America.

SPECIAL GROUPS

Kendrick C. Babcock, *The Scandinavian Element in the United States* (1914). The best treatise on this subject.

Emily Greene Balch, *Our Slavic Fellow Citizens* (1910). A comprehensive study of the Slav in America.

J. M. Campbell, *A History of the Friendly Sons of St. Patrick* (1892).

Mary Roberts Coolidge, *Chinese Immigration* (1909). A sympathetic and detailed account of the Chinaman's experience in America.

A. B. Faust, *The German Element in the United States*. 2 vols. (1909). Like some other books written to prove the vast influence of certain elements of the population, this work is not modest in its claims.

Henry Jones Ford, *The Scotch-Irish in America* (1915).

Lucian J. Fosdick, *The French Blood in America* (1906). Devoted principally to the Huguenot exiles and their descendants.

Charles A. Hanna, *The Scotch-Irish, or the Scot in North Britain, North Ireland, and North America.* 2 vols. (1902).

Eliot Lord, John J. D. Trevor, and Samuel J. Barrows, *The Italian in America* (1905).

T. D'Arcy McGee, *History of the Irish Settlers in North America* (1852).

O. N. Nelson, *History of the Scandinavians and Successful Scandinavians in the United States,* 2 vols. (1900).

J. G. Rosengarten, *French Colonists and Exiles in the United States* (1907). Contains an interesting bibliography of French writings on early American conditions.

UTOPIAS

J. A. Bole, *The Harmony Society* (1904). Besides a concise history of the Rappists, this volume contains many letters and documents illustrative of their customs and business methods.

W. A. Hinds, *American Communities and Cooperative Colonies.* (2d revision 1908.) A useful summary based on personal observations.

G. B. Lockwood, *The New Harmony Communities* (1902). It contains a detailed description of Owen's experiment and interesting details of the Rappists during their sojourn in Indiana.

M. A. Mikkelsen, *The Bishop Hill Colony, A Religious Communistic Settlement in Henry County, Illinois* (1892).

Charles Nordhoff, *The Communistic Societies of the United States* (1875). A description of communities visited by the author.

J. H. Noyes, *History of American Socialisms* (1870).

W. R. Perkins, *History of the Amana Society or Community of True Inspiration* (1891).

E. O. Randall, *History of the Zoar Society* (2d ed. 1900).

Bertha M. Shambaugh, *Amana, the Community of True Inspiration* (1908) gives many interesting details.

Albert Shaw, *Icaria, a Chapter in the History of Communism* (1884). A brilliant account.

INDEX

A. P. A., *see* American Protective Association

Acadia, French in, 18

Adams, J. Q., and Owen, 94

Afghans in United States, 207

Africans, Reed favors exclusion of, 232; *see also* Negroes

Alabama admitted as State (1819), 33

Albany, Shakers settle near, 91; Irish in, 113

Alien and Sedition laws (1798), 221

Amana, 82–84

America, cosmopolitan character, 19–20; American stock, 21 *et seq.*; origin of name, 21–22; now applied to United States, 22; Shakers confined to, 92; "America for Americans," 114; *see also* United States

American Celt, McGee establishes, 120 (note)

American Missionary Association, work with negroes, 58

American party, 114; *see also* Know-Nothing party

American Protective Association, 221–22

Amish, 68 (note)

Anabaptists in Manhattan, 17

Ancient Order of Hibernians, 117

Angell, J. B., on commission to negotiate treaty with China, 198

Antwerp, German emigrants embark at, 134

Arkansas, frontiersmen in, 36; chosen as site by Giessener Gesellschaft, 136; Italians in, 211; Slavs in, 213

Armenians, 184; as laborers, 122; at Granite City (Ill.), 217

Arthur, C. A., and Chinese exclusion act, 199

Asiatics, Pacific coast favors exclusion of, 232; *see also* Orientals

Australia deflects migration to United States, 150

Babcock, K. C., *The Scandinavian Element in the United States*, quoted, 158

Balch, E. G., *Our Slavic Fellow Citizens*, quoted, 164–65; cited, 167 (note), 174

Baltimore, Ephrata draws pupils from, 71; Irish immigrant association, 109; Irish in, 113; Germans in, 127; Italians in, 180; condition of immigrants landing in, 224

Bancroft, George, estimates number of slaves, 47

Barlow, Joel, 151

Bäumeler, *see* Bimeler

Bayard, Nicholas, 16

Beissel, Conrad (or Beizel, or Peysel), 70, 71

Belgians in Charleroi (Penn.), 217